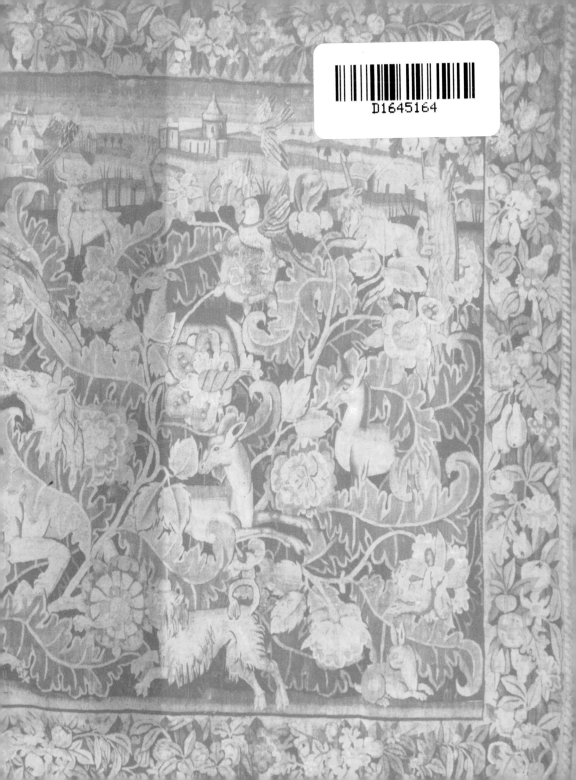

A BOOK OF DELIGHTS

An Anthology of Words and Pictures

'Life,' said a gaunt widow, with a reputation for being clever,—'life is a perpetual toothache'.

In this vein the conversation went on: the familiar topics were discussed, of labour troubles, epidemics, cancer, tuberculosis, and taxation.

Next me there sat a little old lady who was placidly drinking her tea, and taking no part in the melancholy chorus. 'Well, I must say,' she remarked, turning to me, and speaking in an undertone, 'I must say I enjoy life.'

'So do I,' I whispered.

'When I enjoy things,' she went on, 'I know it. Eating, for instance, the sunshine, my hot-water bottle at night. Other people are always thinking of unpleasant things. It makes a difference', she added, as she got up to go with the others.

'All the difference in the world,' I answered.

LOGAN PEARSALL SMITH, *More Trivia*, 1922

A BOOK OF

DELIGHTS

AN ANTHOLOGY

OF WORDS AND PICTURES

COMPILED BY

JOHN HADFIELD

1954

LONDON : HULTON PRESS

FIRST PUBLISHED IN 1954 BY

HULTON PRESS LIMITED

43/44 SHOE LANE

LONDON E.C.4

PRINTED IN GREAT BRITAIN BY

W. S. COWELL LTD

IPSWICH

The frontispiece reproduces
A PORTRAIT OF PAUL SANDBY, R.A.
by FRANCIS COTES, R.A. (*Tate Gallery*)

INTRODUCTION

The world is so full of a number of things,
I'm sure we should all be as happy as kings.

WHEN I WAS A CHILD I was impressed, like many other children, but
also a little puzzled, by Stevenson's familiar lines. I was puzzled by
them only because happiness then seemed to me something unpre-
dictable, not biddable at the command of an 'ought' or a 'should'.
Today, though I have not sunk so deep in pessimism as Dr Johnson's
conclusion that 'the natural flights of the human mind are not from
pleasure to pleasure, but from hope to hope', I realize that happiness
has often to be sought. That it can be found by looking, and can be
cultivated by those who know how, is the conviction in which I have
compiled this anthology.

Another of Dr Johnson's sayings was that 'our brightest blazes of
gladness are commonly kindled by unexpected sparks'. But it would
seem to me a surrender to fatalism, a shameful denial of free will,
to assume that we cannot, whatever our limitations or circumstances,
kindle some warmth of delight from fires which we light ourselves.

Such warmth, I hope, will at least glow and glimmer from the
words and pictures and music which I have brought together in this
book. Although I have inevitably borrowed some of my materials
from those famous anthologies of the pleasures of life compiled by
Mr Martin Armstrong and Miss Rose Macaulay, I have not attempted
as comprehensive a view of my province as they did of theirs. Some
of the supreme examples of pleasure may be missing from these
pages, as will be many of the lesser delights, such as playing cricket
(which I love) or looking at television (which delights me less).

If there is a constant theme—and it is either a very bold or a very
dull anthologist who dares to claim that he has always kept to the

point—it is the *accessibility* of delight, the belief that the greatest happiness can be found in the most common of experiences.

'Man,' wrote Hazlitt, 'is the only animal that laughs and weeps; for he is the only animal that is struck with the difference between what things are and what they ought to be.' This book is not intended as a denial of the existence of pain, sickness, grief, or even the apparently unjustifiable state of melancholy. But it seeks no compromise with the quite indefensible state of *boredom*. I recognize no valid reason for being bored. At any moment, in almost any circumstances not completely governed by pain or grief, it should be possible to see, hear, feel or conjure up in the mind some revelation of delight. That one often fails to do so is a reflection either upon the alertness of one's senses or upon the slothfulness of one's mind.

In the pages which follow I have tried to illustrate, in the context of such common experiences as awakening, loving, dreaming, making (in the sense of *creating*), understanding (in the widest sense of *worshipping*), and falling asleep, the ever-presence of delight, the immanence of happiness. I have also tried to represent, in a series of contrasted passages and pictures, the complementary states of 'being' and 'doing', into which almost all human experience can be divided.

'The race of delight is short', wrote Sir Thomas Browne, 'and pleasures have mutable faces.' The pleasures which show their faces in this book tend, I realize, to be reflective, unspectacular, and solitary. Quite a different book could be built round the delights of activity and society.

This, however, is one man's choice of delights, an even more personal commonplace book than my *Book of Beauty*. Though the prospect which it unfolds may not be everyman's panorama of pleasure, I hope it will at least afford some evidence in support of Vaughan's belief that Heaven lies about us—not only in our infancy, but through all the seven ages of man.

viii

ACKNOWLEDGEMENTS

THE COMPILER AND PUBLISHERS make acknowledgement of the generous facilities afforded by the galleries, museums, artists, photographers, and collectors named in the List of Illustrations. With a few exceptions the works reproduced in colour were specially photographed for this book by Fine Art Engravers, and the compiler wishes to express his appreciation of the care given to this task by the photographers, Mr John Webb and Miss Eileen Tweedy.

For permission to print copyright passages acknowledgement is made to Messrs William Blackwood & Sons for a passage from F. S. Smythe's *Climbs and Ski Runs*; to the Cambridge University Press for two poems by Mr Gerald Bullett; to Messrs Jonathan Cape and the author's widow for two poems by W. H. Davies; to Messrs Cape for a poem from Mr Cecil Day Lewis's *Poems in Wartime*; to Messrs Cape and the trustees for an extract from Samuel Butler's *Note-books*; to Messrs Chatto & Windus for a passage from Mr David Garnett's *A Rabbit in the Air*; to Messrs Chatto & Windus and the author's widow for a poem from Harold Monro's *The Earth for Sale*; to the Clarendon Press for a poem from *Shorter Poems* by Robert Bridges; to Messrs Constable & Company for passages from George Santayana's *Soliloquies in England* and from Logan Pearsall Smith's *Trivia* and *More Trivia*, and a translation by Mr Arthur Waley from *170 Chinese Poems*; to Mr Walter de la Mare, O.M., and Messrs Faber & Faber for two poems and for passages from *Behold, this Dreamer!*, to Messrs J. M. Dent & Sons for poems from Dylan Thomas's *Collected Poems* and Mr Ogden Nash's *Good Intentions*, and for passages from Mr Robert Gibbings's *Coming down the Seine*, M. Norbert Casteret's *Ten Years Under the Earth*, and Joseph Conrad's *Some Reminiscences*; to Mr Robert Graves for a poem from *Fairies and Fusiliers*; to Messrs Hamish Hamilton and Mr Cyril Connolly for passages from *The Unquiet Grave* by 'Palinurus'; to Mr Aldous Huxley and Messrs William Heinemann for a passage from the Introduction to *The Letters of D. H. Lawrence*; to Mrs Lawrence and Messrs Heinemann for a poem from D. H. Lawrence's *Pansies*; to Messrs John Lehmann for a poem from Mr Laurie Lee's *The Bloom of Candles*; to Messrs Longmans Green for a passage from Professor Alexander Findlay's *Chemistry in the Service of Man*; to Messrs Macmillan & Company and Mrs Stephens for a poem from James Stephens's *Collected Poems*; to Messrs Methuen for a poem from G. K. Chesterton's *Collected Poems*; to Dr John Masefield, o.m., and the Society of Authors, for two poems; to Messrs John Murray for a poem from Mr John Betjeman's *Selected Poems*; to Messrs Nicholson & Watson and Miss Kathleen Raine for a poem from *Stone and Flower*; to the Oxford University Press for two poems by W. J. Turner; to Messrs Sidgwick & Jackson for two poems by Rupert Brooke; to Mr Sacheverell Sitwell and Messrs Duckworth & Company for a poem from Mr Sitwell's *Selected Poems*; and to Mr Leonard Woolf for a passage from *A Room of One's Own* by Virginia Woolf.

Acknowledgement is also made for the words and music of 'I will give my love an apple', collected and arranged by Cecil Sharp and Mr Ralph Vaughan Williams, to Messrs Novello & Company; and for the music of the first verse of 'Sleep' by Peter Warlock to the Oxford University Press, who also gave permission for the final bar to be altered for this volume. The compiler is much indebted to Mr Frank Waters for his assistance in the choice of songs and for his setting of the air for the song from *The Beggar's Opera*.

CONTENTS

NOTE. *The reference at the end of each passage is, in almost every instance, to the date and place of its first appearance in book form. The spelling and punctuation of the text has been modernized throughout. In order to allow as much room as possible for the illustrations, notes on their sources are printed at the end of the book.*

ONE can bring no greater reproach against a man than to say that he does not set sufficient value upon pleasure, and there is no greater sign of a fool than the thinking that he can tell at once and easily what it is that pleases him. To know this is not easy, and to extend our knowledge of it is the highest and the most neglected of all arts and branches of education. Indeed, if we could solve the difficulty of knowing what gives us pleasure, if we could find its springs, its inception and earliest *modus operandi*, we should have discovered the secret of life and development.

SAMUEL BUTLER, *Note-books*, 1912

I : AWAKENING

DAY!
Faster and more fast,
O'er night's brim, day boils at last;
Boils, pure gold, o'er the cloud-cup's brim
Where spurting and suppressed it lay,
For not a froth-flake touched the rim
Of yonder gap in the solid gray
Of the eastern cloud, an hour away;
But forth one wavelet, then another, curled,
Till the whole sunrise, not to be suppressed,
Rose, reddened, and its seething breast
Flickered in bounds, grew gold, then overflowed the world.

ROBERT BROWNING, from 'Pippa Passes'
Bells and Pomegranates, 1841

So have I seen the sun kiss the frozen earth which was bound up
with the images of death and the colder breath of the North; and
then the waters break from their enclosures, and melt with joy, and
run in useful channels; and the flies do rise again from their little
graves in walls and dance a while in the air, to tell that there is joy
within and that the great mother of creatures will open the stock of
her new refreshment, become useful to mankind, and sing praises to
her Redeemer.

JEREMY TAYLOR, *Twenty-five Sermons*, 1653

13

A NEW DAY

SLOW bleak awakening from the morning dream
Brings me in contact with the sudden day.
I am alive—this I.
I let my fingers move along my body.
Realization warns them, and my nerves
Prepare their rapid messages and signals.
While Memory begins recording, coding,
Repeating; all the time Imagination
Mutters; You'll only die.

Here's a new day. O Pendulum move slowly!
My usual clothes are waiting on their peg.
I am alive—this I.
And in a moment Habit, like a crane,
Will bow its neck and dip its pulleyed cable,
Gathering me, my body, and our garment,
And swing me forth, oblivious of my question,
Into the daylight—why?

I think of all the others who awaken,
And wonder if they go to meet the morning
More valiantly than I;
Nor asking of this Day they will be living:
What have I done that I should be alive?
O, can I not forget that I am living?
How shall I reconcile the two conditions:
Living, and yet—to die?

Between the curtains the autumnal sunlight
With lean and yellow finger points me out;
The clock moans: Why? Why? Why?
But suddenly, as if without a reason,
Heart, Brain and Body, and Imagination
All gather in tumultuous joy together,
Running like children down the path of morning
To fields where they can play without a quarrel:
A country I'd forgotten, but remember,
And welcome with a cry.

O cool glad pasture; living tree, tall corn,
Great cliff, or languid sloping sand, cold sea,
Waves; rivers curving: you, eternal flowers,
Give me content, while I can think of you:
Give me your living breath!
Back to your rampart, Death.

HAROLD MONRO
'Living', *The Earth for Sale*, 1928

THE happiest part of a man's life is what he
passes lying awake in bed in the morning.

SAMUEL JOHNSON
in Boswell's *Life*, 1791

MORNING GLORY

THE water sparkles as I pour,
Each drop a crystal gem,
Each several drop a gleaming world
Lost in the clear containing glass
Or in the basin lying sleek and still.
What richness!—when a man may slake
His sleepy thirst with precious gems,
And among shining planets plunge his hands.

GERALD BULLETT, *Poems*, 1949

AN WASHING: PASTEL DRAWING BY EDGAR DEGAS, *c.* 1890

ROSE IN MORNING DEW: PHOTOGRAPH BY CLARENCE PONTING

DEW

SEE how the Orient dew,
Shed from the bosom of the morn
   Into the blowing roses,
Yet careless of its mansion new—
For the clear region where t'was born
   Round in itself encloses
And, in its little globe's extent,
Frames as it can its native element—
   How it the purple flower does slight,
     Scarce touching where it lies,
But, gazing back upon the skies,
   Shines with a mournful light,
     Like its own tear,
Because so long divided from the Sphere.

Restless it rolls, and unsecure,
Trembling lest it grow impure,
Till the warm sun pity its pain,
And to the skies exhale it back again.
   So the soul, that drop, that ray
Of the clear fountain of eternal day,
   Could it within the human flower be seen,
     Remembering still its former height,
Shuns the sweet leaves and blossoms green,
   And, recollecting its own light,
Does, in its pure and circling thoughts, express
The greater heaven in a heaven less.

ANDREW MARVELL
Miscellaneous Poems, 1681

RENEWAL

THE fringëd vallance of your eyes advance,
Shake off your canopied and downy trance;
Phoebus already quaffs the morning dew,
Each does his daily lease of life renew.
He darts his beams on the lark's mossy house,
And from his quiet tenement does rouse
The little, charming, and harmonious fowl,
Which sings its lump of body to a soul:
Swiftly it clambers up in the steep air
With warbling throat, and makes each note a stair.
This the solicitous lover straight alarms,
Who too long slumbered in his Celia's arms:
And now the swelling spunges of the night
With aching heads stagger from their delight:
Slovenly tailors to their needles haste:
Already now the moving shops are placed
By those who crop the treasures of the fields
And all those gems the ripening summer yields.

THOMAS SHADWELL
Timon of Athens, 1678

LARK RISE

THE lark now leaves his watery nest
   And climbing shakes his dewy wings:
He takes this window for the east,
   And to implore your light he sings,
Awake, awake! the morn will never rise
Till she can dress her beauty at your eyes.

The merchant bows unto the seaman's star,
   The ploughman from the sun his season takes;
But still the lover wonders what they are
   Who look for day before his mistress wakes.
Awake, awake! break through your veils of lawn;
Then draw your curtains, and begin the dawn.

SIR WILLIAM DAVENANT, *Works*, 1673
(written before 1656)

WHAT if the lark does carol in the sky,
   Soaring beyond the sight to find him out—
Wherefore am I to rise at such a fly?
   I'm not a trout.

THOMAS HOOD, from 'Morning Meditations'
in *The Amaranth*, 1839

DAWN CHORUS

This morning, lying couched amid the grass
In the deep, deep dingle south of Llangwyth's Pass,
   While it was yet neither quite bright nor dark,
I heard a new and wonderful High Mass.
   The Chief Priest was the nightingale: the lark
And thrush assisted him: and some small bird
   (I do not weet his name) acted as Clerk.
My spirit was lapped in ecstasy: each word,
Word after word, thrilled through me like the deep
Rich music of a dream: not wholly asleep
Nor all awake was I, but, as it were,
   Tranced somewhere between one state and the other.
   All heavy thoughts that through the long day smother
Man's heart and soul with weariness and care
   Were gone, and in their place reigned pure delight.
   The nightingale, sent from a far and bright
Land by my golden sister, prophesied
   Of blessëd days to come, in a sweet voice:
   And the small bird, responding, sang 'Rejoice, rejoice!'
I heard his little bill tinkle and jingle
With a clear silver sound that filled the dingle.
Heaven is a state wherein bliss and devotion mingle,
   And such was mine this morn: I could have died
Of rapture . . .

DAVID AP GWYLYM (fourteenth century) rendered
by JAMES CLARENCE MANGAN, *Poems,* 1903

APRIL RISE

If ever I saw blessing in the air
    I see it now in this still early day
Where lemon-green the vaporous morning drips
    Wet sunlight on the powder of my eye.

Blown bubble-film of blue, the sky wraps round
    Weeds of warm light whose every root and rod
Splutters with soapy green, and all the world
    Sweats with the bead of summer in its bud.

If ever I heard blessing it is there
    Where birds in trees that shoals and shadows are
Splash with their hidden wings and drops of sound
    Break on my ears their crests of throbbing air.

Pure in the haze the emerald sun dilates,
    The lips of sparrows milk the mossy stones,
While white as water by the lake a girl
    Swims her green hand among the gathered swans.

Now, as the almond burns its smoking wick,
    Dropping small flames to light the candled grass;
Now, as my low blood scales its second chance,
    If ever world were blessed, now it is.

LAURIE LEE, *The Bloom of Candles*, 1947

23

FIRST JOYS

Born to the world with my hands clenched,
  I wept and shut my eyes;
Into my mouth a breast was forced,
  To stop my bitter cries.
I did not know—nor cared to know—
  A woman from a man;
Until I saw a sudden light,
  And all my joys began.

From that great hour my hands went forth,
  And I began to prove
That many a thing my two eyes saw
  My hands had power to move:
My fingers now began to work,
  And all my toes likewise;
And reaching out with fingers stretched,
  I laughed, with open eyes.

w. h. davies, 'Infancy'
The Bird of Paradise, 1914

ROMILLY SEATED: DRAWING BY AUGUSTUS JOHN, R.A.

HOW LIKE AN ANGEL

How like an angel came I down!
  How bright are all things here!
When first among his works I did appear
  Oh, how their glory did me crown!
The world resembled his eternity,
  In which my soul did walk;
And everything that I did see
  Did with me talk . . .

A native health and innocence
  Within my bones did grow,
And while my God did all his glories show,
  I felt a vigour in my sense
That was all spirit: I within did flow
  With seas of life like wine;
I nothing in the world did know.
  But 'twas divine . . .

For property itself was mine
  And hedges, ornaments;
Walls, houses, coffers, and their rich contents,
  To make me rich combine.
Clothes, costly jewels, laces, I esteemed
  My wealth by others worn;
For me they all to wear them seemed
  When I was born.

THOMAS TRAHERNE
Poems of Felicity, 1903, written *c.* 1670
(other verses of this poem will be found on page 128)

MORNING IMAGES

I SEE the wild flowers, in their summer morn
   Of beauty, feeding on joy's luscious hours;
The gay convolvulus, wreathing round the thorn,
   Agape for honey showers;
And slender kingcup, burnished with the dew
   Of morning's early hours,
      Like gold yminted new . . .

I love at early morn, from new mown swath,
   To see the startled frog his route pursue,
And mark while, leaping o'er the dripping path,
   His bright sides scatter dew;
And early lark that from its bustle flies
   To hail his matin new;
      And watch him to the skies:

To note on hedgerow baulks, in moisture sprent,
   The jetty snail creep from the mossy thorn,
With earnest heed, and tremulous intent,
   Frail brother of the morn,
That from the tiny bents and misted leaves
   Withdraws his timid horn,
      And fearful vision weaves:

Or swallow heed on smoke-tanned chimney top,
　Wont to be first unsealing morning's eye,
Ere yet the bee hath gleaned one wayward drop
　Of honey on his thigh;
To see him seek morn's airy couch to sing,
　Until the golden sky
　　Bepaint his russet wing.

Or sauntering boy by tanning corn espy,
　With clapping noise to startle birds away,
And hear him bawl to every passer by
　To know the hour of day;
While the uncradled breezes, fresh and strong,
　With waking blossoms play,
　　And breathe Æolian song . . .

Rich music breathes in Summer's every sound;
　And in her harmony of varied greens,
Woods, meadows, hedge-rows, corn-fields, all around
　Much beauty intervenes,
Filling with harmony the ear and eye,
　While o'er the mingling scenes
　　Far spreads the laughing sky . . .

JOHN CLARE, from 'Summer Images'
The Rural Muse, 1835

29

UNDER THE APPLE BOUGHS

Now as I was young and easy under the apple boughs
About the lilting house and happy as the grass was green,
    The night above the dingle starry,
        Time let me hail and climb
    Golden in the heydays of his eyes,
And honoured among wagons I was prince of the apple towns
And once below a time I lordly had the trees and leaves
        Trail with daisies and barley
    Down the rivers of the windfall light.

And as I was green and carefree, famous among the barns
About the happy yard and singing as the farm was home,
    In the sun that is young once only,
        Time let me play and be
    Golden in the mercy of his means.
And green and golden I was huntsman and herdsman, the calves
Sang to my horn, the foxes on the hills barked clear and cold,
        And the sabbath rang slowly
    In the pebbles of the holy streams.

All the sun long it was running, it was lovely, the hay
Fields high as the house, the tunes from the chimneys, it was air
    And playing, lovely and watery
        And fire green as grass.
    And nightly under the simple stars
As I rode to sleep the owls were bearing the farm away,
All the moon long I heard, blessed among stables, the nightjars
        Flying with the ricks, and the horses
           Flashing into the dark.

And then to awake, and the farm, like a wanderer white
With the dew, come back, the cock on his shoulder: it was all
    Shining, it was Adam and maiden,
        The sky gathered again
    And the sun grew round that very day.
So it must have been after the birth of the simple light
In the first, spinning place, the spellbound horses walking warm
    Out of the whinnying green stable
        On to the fields of praise.

And honoured among foxes and pheasants by the gay house
Under the new made clouds and happy as the heart was long,
    In the sun born over and over,
        I ran my heedless ways,
    My wishes raced through the house high hay
And nothing I cared, at my sky blue trades, that time allows
In all his tuneful turning so few and such morning songs
    Before the children green and golden
        Follow him out of grace.

Nothing I cared, in the lamb white days, that time would take me
Up to the swallow thronged loft by the shadow of my hand,
    In the moon that is always rising,
        Nor that riding to sleep
    I should hear him fly with the high fields
And wake to the farm forever fled from the childless land.
Oh as I was young and easy in the mercy of his means,
        Time held me green and dying
    Though I sang in my chains like the sea.

DYLAN THOMAS, 'Fern Hill'
Deaths and Entrances, 1946

WHEN on a summer's morn I wake,
  And open my two eyes,
Out to the clear, born-singing rills
  My bird-like spirit flies.

To hear the Blackbird, Cuckoo, Thrush,
  Or any bird in song;
And common leaves that hum all day,
  Without a throat or tongue.

And when Time strikes the hour for sleep,
  Back in my room alone,
My heart has many a sweet bird's song—
  And one that's all my own.

W. H. DAVIES
The Bird of Paradise, 1914

II : DELIGHTS OF THE SENSES

By the very right of your senses you enjoy the world. Is not the beauty of the Hemisphere present to your eye? Doth not the glory of the sun pay tribute to your sight? Is not the vision of the world an amiable thing? Do not the stars shed influences to perfect the air? Is not that a marvellous body to breathe in? To visit the lungs, repair the spirits, revive the senses, cool the blood, fill the empty spaces between the earth and heavens, and yet give liberty to all objects?

> THOMAS TRAHERNE
> *Centuries of Meditations*, 1908 (written *c.* 1670)

The tree which moves some to tears of joy is in the eyes of others only a green thing which stands in the way . . . As a man is, so he sees.

> WILLIAM BLAKE

To a lady who, looking at an engraving of a house, called it an ugly thing, he said, 'No, madam, there is nothing ugly; I never saw an ugly thing in my life: for let the form of an object be what it may—light, shade, and perspective will always make it beautiful.'

> JOHN CONSTABLE
> quoted in C. R. LESLIE's *Life*, 1843

MIRRORS IN MINIATURE

THERE is not so poor a creature, but may be thy glass to see God in. The greatest flat glass that can be made cannot represent anything greater than it is. If every gnat that flies were an Archangel, all that could but tell me that there is a God; and the poorest worm that creeps tells me that.

JOHN DONNE

THE sweetest essences are always confined in the smallest glasses.

JOHN DRYDEN

THE blessed Francis being in his cell at Santa Maria di Porziuncola, there was a grasshopper making a great singing upon a fig-tree. And many times he said to her: Well done! Praise the Lord! And at last he called her; and instantly, as if bidden by God, she came upon his hand, and the blessed Francis said to her: Sing, my sister. And she sang. And then he said: Sing no more. And she went to a place near by, and for full eight days she stayed there singing, and the blessed Francis said: Let us now give our sister grasshopper leave to depart, for she has afforded us much refreshment. And instantly, receiving his permission, she departed and returned no more, as if she dared not to transgress his commandment.

SAINT BONAVENTURA

THERE is nothing, sir, too little for so little a creature as man. It is by studying little things that we attain the great art of having as little misery and as much happiness as possible.

SAMUEL JOHNSON

FLOWERS AND INSECTS: PAINTING BY ROELANDT SAVERY 1611

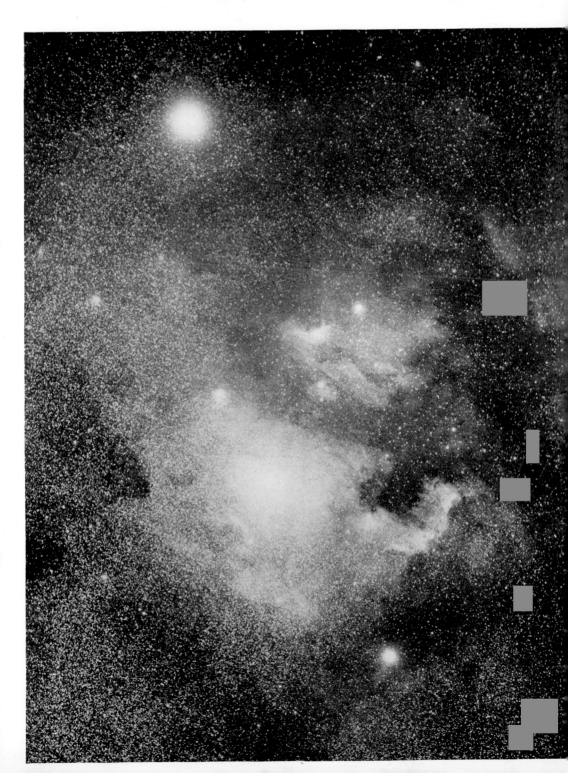

STARS

IF the stars should appear one night in a thousand years, how would men believe and adore; and preserve for many generations the remembrance of the city of God which had been shown! But every night come out these envoys of beauty, and light the universe with their admonishing smile.

RALPH WALDO EMERSON, *Nature*, 1836

. . . LOOK how the floor of heaven
Is thick inlaid with patines of bright gold!
There's not the smallest orb which thou behold'st
But in his motion like an angel sings
Still quiring to the young-eyed cherubins.

WILLIAM SHAKESPEARE
The Merchant of Venice, 1595

WHEN I survey the bright
   Celestial sphere,
So rich with jewels hung, that night
Doth like an Ethiop bride appear,

My soul her wings doth spread
   And heavenward flies,
Th' Almighty's mysteries to read
In the large volumes of the skies . . .

WILLIAM HABINGTON, *Castara*, 1640

37

THE UPWARD GLANCE

'Up among those top leaves, what do you see,
High as our zenith, or our apogee?
I am holding the ladder foot, lest you fall;
Call down loud, and tell me all!'
I stood by the rungs quite still, to hear
And watched his scissors trim and shear:
His voice rings through the leaves so cool
Between these clippings thick as wool.
'I have all the blossoms near me
Where I stand now—Can you hear me?—
All the blossoms, all the flowers
I see as from a hundred towers:
Wisps of wool, or flakes of snow
Are but petals I let go.
This branch is like my window-ledge
High in the eaves where young birds fledge;
Perhaps I'll find the wind's soft nest,
Lined with feathers from her breast—
Or would you like a white flower best?'—
'Do not take her dappled egg:
Do not shake her nest, I beg:
Bring me down a flower instead,
Soft as milk, and white as bread.'
He climbs the tree-stem like a mast:
He shouts, 'Now hold my ladder fast!'
I held it while he clipped the stem
Pulling the leaves to cut at them—

Now he's climbing down, it seems,
A stairway built of sun's bright beams
In timbers, straight and strong, of gold
Sloped like the ladder that I hold.
He says, 'Here is the flower I've cut.'
I take it, thank him, smell it, but,
Thinking why his path was lit,
I hear the sun explaining it.
'This man knows where the wind's nest lies
In thinnest branches near the skies:
He never shook it, never tried,
To steal the eggs that lay inside;
So she holds still the boughs, and I
Gild his ladder from on high;
The flower he gives into your hand
Is sweet as honey, gold as sand—
If either of you climb again,
No wind will blow, I'll send no rain;
She'll flash for you her feathers bright
And I will keep you in my sight,
Like golden stars you'll walk up here,
And shine among us, free from fear!'

SACHEVERELL SITWELL, 'Magnolia Tree'
The Thirteenth Caesar, and Other Poems, 1924

NATURE'S ART

The fields are green, the spring grows on apace,
    And Nature's art begins to take the air;
Each herb her scent, each flower doth show her grace,
    And beauty braggeth of her bravest fair.
The lambs and rabbits sweetly run at base;
    The fowls do plume, and fishes fall to play;
The muses all have chose a sitting place
    To sing and play the shepherd's roundelay . . .
The little wren that never sung a note
    Is peeping now to prove how she can sing;
The nightingale hath set in tune her throat,
    And all the woods with little robins ring.
Love is abroad as naked as my nail,
    And little birds do flicker from their nests;
Diana sweet hath set aside her veil,
    And Phillis shows the beauty of her breasts.
O blessèd breasts, the beauty of the spring!
    O blessèd spring, that such a beauty shows!
Of highest trees the holly is the king,
    And of all flowers fair fall the queen, the rose!

NICHOLAS BRETON, British Museum MS.

YOUNG GIRL BATHING: PAINTING BY PIERRE AUGUSTE RENOIR, 1892

LES PEUPLIERS: PAINTING BY CLAUDE MONET, 1890

SKY

. . . Look overhead
How air is azurëd;
O how! nay do but stand
Where you can lift your hand
Skywards: rich, rich it laps
Round the four fingergaps.
Yet such a sapphire-shot,
Charged, steepëd sky will not
Stain light.   Yea, mark you this:
It does no prejudice.
The glass-blue days are those
When every colour glows,
Each shape and shadow shows.
Blue be it: this blue heaven
The seven or seven times seven
Hued sunbeam will transmit
Perfect, not alter it.
Or if there does some soft,
On things aloof, aloft,
Bloom breathe, that one breath more
Earth is the fairer for . . .

GERARD MANLEY HOPKINS
Poems, 1930 (written 1883)

THE HEAT OF THE SUN

I NEVER wholly feel that summer is high,
However green the trees, or loud the birds,
However movelessly eye-winking herds
Stand in field ponds, or under large trees lie,
Till I do climb all cultured pastures by,
That hedged by hedgerows studiously fretted trim,
Smile like a lady's face with lace laced prim,
And on some moor or hill that seeks the sky
Lonely and nakedly,—utterly lie down,
And feel the sunshine throbbing on body and limb,
My drowsy brain in pleasant drunkenness swim,
Each rising thought sink back and dreamily drown,
Smiles creep o'er my face, and smother my lips, and cloy,
Each muscle sink to itself, and separately enjoy.

EBENEZER JONES, 'High Summer'
Studies of Sensation and Event, 1843

THE LIGHT OF THE MOON

... AFTER dining in the Place St. Michel, I wandered along the quay towards Notre-Dame. The cathedral was floodlit, ivory white against a purple sky. The glare of the lamps threw into clear relief the traceries of walls and windows, cast ghostly shadows among the many buttresses. Suddenly behind the colonnade between the towers there showed a golden arc. As quickly as it had appeared it climbed, until, a perfect sphere, the moon hung high in the heavens behind the tall shadowed spire. Normally one thinks of moonlight as silver and cold, but that night it was golden and warm. Glowing and alive, it moved upwards through the sky: the church beneath it was ashen white, immobile, built as it were of dry bones. It was no longer a solid structure; it seemed a façade, a skeleton of itself painted on a dark backcloth. Overhead the moon rose higher and higher in the firmament. It poured its gold into the river, and the lamps on the bridges added faint echoes to its lustre. Lovers under the arches ceased a moment from their embracing; *clochards* turned on their hard beds and glanced upwards, while in the street above them from all the moving traffic heads craned to glimpse this giant sunflower of the night.

ROBERT GIBBINGS
Coming Down the Seine, 1953

45

EARTH'S EMBROIDERY

FOR if delight may provoke men's labour, what greater delight is there than to behold the earth apparalled with plants, as with a robe of embroidered work, set with Orient pearls and garnished with great diversity of rare and costly jewels? If this variety and perfection of colours may affect the eye, it is such in herbs and flowers that no Apelles, no Zeuxis, ever could by any art express the like: if odours or if taste may work satisfaction they are both so sovereign in plants and so comfortable that no confection of the apothecaries can equal their excellent virtue. But these delights are in the outward senses; the principal delight is in the mind, singularly enriched with the knowledge of these visible things, setting forth to us the invisible wisdom and admirable workmanship of Almighty God.

JOHN GERARD, from the
Dedication of his *Herbal*, 1597.

FLOWERS, FRUIT AND OYSTERS: PAINTING BY JAN DAVIDZ DE HEEM

THE NARROW PERSPECTIVE

GOD is glorified in the sun and moon, in the rare fabric of the honeycombs, in the discipline of bees, in the economy of pismires, in the little houses of birds, in the curiosity of an eye, God being pleased to delight in those little images and reflexes of himself from those pretty mirrors, which like a crevice in a wall through a narrow perspective transmit the species of a vast excellency . . .

JEREMY TAYLOR, *Twenty-eight Sermons*, 1651

PLEASURES lie thickest where no pleasures seem;
There's not a leaf that falls upon the ground
But holds some joy, of silence or of sound,
Some sprite begotten of a summer dream.
The very meanest things are made supreme
With innate ecstasy. No grain of sand
But moves a bright and million-peopled land,
And hath its Edens and its Eves, I deem.

SAMUEL LAMAN BLANCHARD, *Lyric Offerings*, 1828

VOICES

A FEW strokes brought us alongside, and it was then that, for the very first time in my life, I heard myself addressed in English—the speech of my secret choice, of my future, of long friendships, of the deepest affections, of hours of toil and hours of ease, and of solitary hours too, of books read, of thoughts pursued, of remembered emotions—of my very dreams! And if (after being thus fashioned by it in that part of me which cannot decay) I dare not claim it aloud as my own, then, at any rate the speech of my children. Thus small events grow memorable by the passage of time. As to the quality of the address itself I cannot say it was very striking. Too short for eloquence, and devoid of all charm of tone, it consisted precisely of the three words, 'Look out there', growled out huskily above my head.

JOSEPH CONRAD, *Some Reminiscences*, 1912

WHEN I but hear her sing, I fare
Like one that, raisëd, holds his ear
To some bright star in the supremest round;
Through which, besides the light that's seen,
There may be heard, from heaven within,
The rests of anthems that the angels sound.

OWEN FELLTHAM, *Lusoria*, 1661

ECHOES

THERE was a boy; ye knew him well, ye cliffs
And islands of Winander!—many a time,
At evening, when the earliest stars began
To move along the edges of the hills,
Rising or setting, would he stand alone,
Beneath the trees, or by the glimmering lake;
And there, with fingers interwoven, both hands
Pressed closely palm to palm and to his mouth
Uplifted, he, as through an instrument,
Blew mimic hootings to the silent owls,
That they might answer him. And they would shout
Across the watery vale, and shout again,
Responsive to his call, with quivering peals,
And long halloos, and screams, and echoes loud
Redoubled and redoubled; concourse wild
Of jocund din! And when a lengthened pause
Of silence came and baffled his best skill,
Then, sometimes, in that silence, while he hung
Listening, a gentle shock of mild surprise
Has carried far into his heart the voice
Of mountain torrents; or the visible scene
Would enter unawares into his mind
With all its solemn imagery, its rocks,
Its woods, and that uncertain heaven, received
Into the bosom of the steady lake.

WILLIAM WORDSWORTH, *The Prelude*, 1850
(written 1799–1805)

'AN DIE MUSIK'   WORDS BY FRANZ VON SCHOBER

MUSIC BY FRANZ SCHUBERT

MUSIC

WHEN music sounds, gone is the earth I know,
And all her lovely things even lovelier grow;
Her flowers in vision flame, her forest trees
Lift burdened branches, stilled with ecstasies.

When music sounds, out of the water rise
Naiads whose beauty dims my waking eyes,
Rapt in strange dream burns each enchanted face,
With solemn echoing stirs their dwelling-place.

When music sounds, all that I was I am
Ere to this haunt of brooding dust I came;
And from Time's woods break into distant song
The swift-winged hours, as I hasten along.

WALTER DE LA MARE, *Motley*, 1918

HARMONY

When whispering strains, with creeping wind,
  Distil soft passion through the heart;
And when at every touch we find
  Our pulses beat and bear a part;
    When threads can make
    A heart-string shake,
    Philosophy
    Can not deny
  Our souls consist of harmony.

When unto heavenly joys, we feign
  Whate'er the soul affecteth most,
Which only thus we can explain,
  By music of the heavenly host,
    Whose lays, methinks,
    Make stars to shrink,
    Philosophy
    May judge thereby
  Our souls consist of harmony.

Oh, lull me, lull me, charming air!
  My senses rock with wonder sweet;
Like snow on wool thy fallings are,
  Soft as a spirit's are thy feet;
    Grief who need fear
    That hath an ear?
    Down let him lie
    And slumbering die,
And change his soul for harmony.

WILLIAM STRODE, in *The Academy of Compliments*, 1650

THE CHIME OF THE SEA

CONSIDER the sea's listless chime:
  Time's self it is, made audible,
  The murmur of the earth's own shell.
Secret continuance sublime
  Is the sea's end: our sight may pass
  No furlong further. Since time was,
This sound hath told the lapse of time.

No quiet, which is death's,—it hath
  The mournfulness of ancient life,
  Enduring always at dull strife.
As the world's heart of rest and wrath,
  Its painful pulse is in the sands.
  Last utterly, the whole sky stands,
Grey and not known, along its path . .

Gather a shell from the strown beach
  And listen at its lips: they sigh
  The same desire and mystery,
The echo of the whole sea's speech.
  And all mankind is thus at heart
  Not anything but what thou art:
And Earth, Sea, Man, are all in each.

DANTE GABRIEL ROSSETTI
from 'The Sea's Limits, *Poems*, 1870

SEA
PHOTOGRAPH BY EDWIN

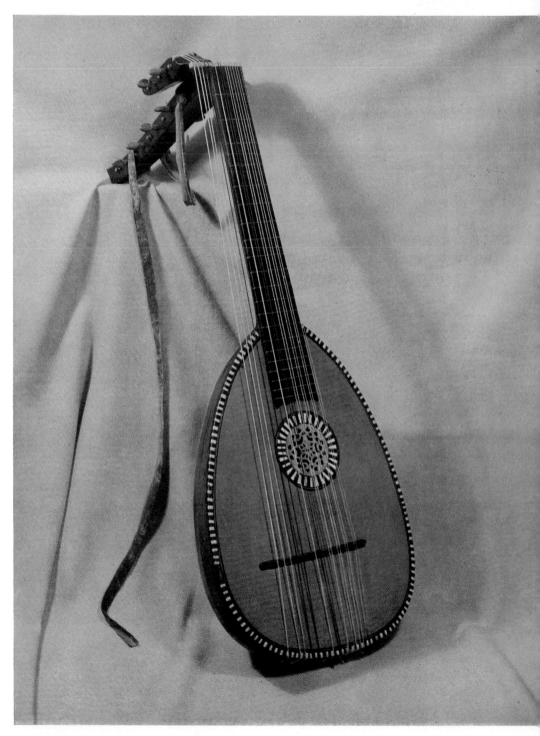

FRENCH LUTE: SEVENTEENTH CENTURY

THE LUTE SPEAKS

WHILST vital sap did make me spring,
And leaf and bough did flourish brave,
I then was dumb and could not sing,
Nor had the voice which now I have:
But when the axe my life did end
The Muses nine this voice did send.

EDMUND SPENSER
'Verses upon the Earl of Cork's Lute'
A View of the State of Ireland, 1633

BREAKFAST

THE divine took his seat at the breakfast-table, and began to compose his spirits by the gentle sedative of a large cup of tea, the demulcent of a well-buttered muffin, and the tonic of a small lobster.

The Rev. Dr. Folliott. You are a man of taste, Mr. Crotchet. A man of taste is seen at once in the array of his breakfast-table. It is the foot of Hercules, the far-shining face of the great work, according to Pindar's doctrine:

> Far-shining be the face
> Of a great work begun.

The breakfast is the *prosopon* of the great work of the day. Chocolate, coffee, tea, cream, eggs, ham, tongue, cold fowl—all these are good, and bespeak good knowledge in him who sets them forth: but the touchstone is fish: anchovy is the first step, prawns and shrimps the second; and I laud him who reaches even to these: potted char and lampreys are the third, and a fine stretch of progression; but lobster is, indeed, matter for a May morning, and demands a rare combination of knowledge and virtue in him who sets it forth.

THOMAS LOVE PEACOCK
Crotchet Castle, 1831

LUNCHEON

THE lunch on this occasion began with soles, sunk in a deep dish, over which the college cook had spread a counterpane of the whitest cream, save that it was branded here and there with brown spots like the spots on the flanks of a doe. After that came the partridges, but if this suggests a couple of bald, brown birds on a plate you are mistaken. The partridges, many and various, came with all their retinue of sauces and salads, the sharp and the sweet, each in its order; their potatoes, thin as coins but not so hard; their sprouts, foliated as rosebuds but more succulent. And no sooner had the roast and its retinue been done with than the silent serving-man, the Beadle himself perhaps in a milder manifestation, set before us, wreathed in napkins, a confection which rose all sugar from the waves. To call it pudding and so relate it to rice and tapioca would be an insult. Meanwhile the wineglasses had flushed yellow and flushed crimson; had been emptied; had been filled. And thus by degrees was lit, halfway down the spine, which is the seat of the soul, not that hard little electric light which we call brilliance, as it pops in and out upon our lips, but the more profound, subtle and subterranean glow which is the rich yellow flame of rational intercourse. No need to hurry. No need to sparkle. No need to be anybody but oneself. We are all going to heaven and Vandyck is of the company—in other words, how good life seemed, how sweet its rewards, how trivial this grudge or that grievance, how admirable friendship and the society of one's kind, as, lighting a good cigarette, one sunk among the cushions in the window-seat.

VIRGINIA WOOLF, *A Room of One's Own*, 1929

DINNER

SIR, respect your dinner, idolize it, enjoy it properly. You will be by many hours in the week, many weeks in the year, and many years in your life, the happier if you do.

Don't tell me it is not worthy of a man. All a man's senses are worthy of employment, and should be cultivated as a duty. The senses are the arts. What glorious feasts does Nature prepare for your eye in animal form, in landscape and in painting! Are you to put out your eyes and not see? What royal dishes does her bounty provide for you in the shape of poetry, music, whether windy or wiry, notes of the human voice, or ravishing songs of birds! Are you to stuff your ears with cotton, and vow that the sense of hearing is unmanly?—you obstinate dolt you! No, surely; nor must you be so absurd as to fancy that the art of eating is in any way less worthy than the other two. You like your dinner, man! never be ashamed to say so. If you don't like your victuals, pass on to the next article; but remember that every man who has been worth a fig in this world as poet, painter, or musician, has had a good appetite, and a good taste.

WILLIAM MAKEPEACE THACKERAY
'Memorials of Gormandising'
in *Fraser's Magazine*, June 1841

KEATS ON CLARET

Now I like claret—Whenever I can have claret, I must drink it. 'Tis the only palate affair that I am at all sensual in. Would it not be a good speck to send you some vine-roots? Could it be done? I'll enquire. If you could make some wine like claret, to drink on summer evenings in an arbour! For really 'tis so fine. It fills one's mouth with a gushing freshness, then goes down cool and feverless: then, you do not feel it quarrelling with your liver. No; 'tis rather a peacemaker, and lies as quiet as it did in the grape. Then it is as fragrant as the Queen Bee, and the more ethereal part of it mounts into the brain, not assaulting the cerebral apartments, like a bully in a bad house looking for his trull, and hurrying from door to door, bouncing against the wainscot, but rather walks like Aladdin about his enchanted palace, so gently that you do not feel his step.

JOHN KEATS, Letter, Feb. 18, 1819

FALSTAFF ON SHERRY

A GOOD sherris-sack hath a two-fold operation in it. It ascends me into the brain; dries me there all the foolish and dull and crudy vapours which environ it; makes it apprehensive, quick, forgetive, full of nimble, fiery and delectable shapes; which, delivered o'er to the voice, the tongue, which is the birth, becomes excellent wit. The second property of your excellent sherris is, the warming of the blood; which before, cold and settled, left the liver white and pale, which is the badge of pusillanimity and cowardice; but the sherris warms it and makes it course from the inwards to the parts extreme: it illumineth the face, which as a beacon gives warning to all the rest of this little kingdom, man, to arm; and then the vital commoners and inland petty spirits muster me all to their captain, the heart, who, great and puffed up with this retinue, doth any deed of courage; and this valour comes of sherris, so that skill in the weapon is nothing without sack, for that sets it a-work; and learning a mere hoard of gold kept by a devil, till sack commences it and sets it in act and use.

WILLIAM SHAKESPEARE
King Henry IV, Part II, 1600

ROGER SWIZZLE ON DIET

'You see, Sir Harry', he would say, 'it's all done by eating. More people dig their graves with their teeth than we imagine. Not that I would deny you the good things of this world, but I would recommend a few at a time, and no mixing. No side dishes. No liqueurs —only two or three wines. Whatever your stomach fancies, give it. Begin now, tomorrow, with the waters. A pint before breakfast— half an hour after, tea, fried ham, and eggs, brown bread, and a walk. Luncheon—another pint—a roast pigeon and fried potatoes, then a ride. Dinner at six, not later, mind; gravy soup, glass of sherry, nice fresh turbot and lobster sauce—wouldn't recommend salmon—another glass of sherry—then a good cut out of the middle of a well-browned saddle of mutton, wash it over with a few glasses of iced champagne; and if you like a little light pastry to wind up with, well and good. A pint of old port and a devilled biscuit can hurt no man. Mind, no salads, or cucumbers, or celery, at dinner, or fruit after. Turtle soup is very wholesome, so is venison. Don't let the punch be too acid though. Drink the water, live on a regimen, and you'll be well in no time.'

With these and suchlike comfortable assurances, he pocketed his guineas and bowed his patients out by the dozen.

ROBERT SMITH SURTEES
Handley Cross, 1843

SMELLS

AND because the breath of flowers is far sweeter in the air (where it comes and goes, like the warbling of music) than in the hand, therefore nothing is more fit for that delight than to know what be the flowers and plants that do best perfume the air ... That which, above all others, yields the sweetest smell in the air is the Violet ... Next to that is the Musk-Rose; then the Strawberry leaves dying with a most excellent cordial smell; then the flowers of the vines—it is a little dust, like the dust of a bent, which grows upon the cluster in the first coming forth. Then Sweet Briar; then Wallflowers, which are very delightful to be set under a parlour or lower chamber window; then Pinks and Gilliflowers, specially the matted Pink, and Clove Gilliflower; then the flowers of the Lime Tree; then the Honeysuckles, so they be somewhat afar off. Of Bean flowers I speak not, because they are fieldflowers. But those which perfume the air most delightfully, not passed by as the rest, but being trodden upon and crushed, are three—that is Burnet, Wild Thyme, and Water Mints. Therefore you are to set whole alleys of them, to have the pleasure, when you walk or tread.

FRANCIS BACON, BARON VERULAM, *Essays*, 1625

... Some putrifactions and excrements do yield excellent odours: as civis and musk, and, as some think, ambergris ... The senses love not to be over-pleased, but to have a commixture of somewhat that is in itself ingrate. Certainly we see how discords in music, falling upon concords, make the sweetest strains; and we see again what strange tastes delight the taste, as red herrings, caviare, parmesan, &c. And it may be the same holdeth in smells.

FRANCIS BACON, BARON VERULAM, *Sylva Sylvarum*, 1669

POM
AND VINAIC
PHOTOGRAPH BY EDWIN

TOBY JUG BY RALPH WOOD, 'THE SQUIRE', c. 1770

A PIPE OF TOBACCO

LITTLE tube of mighty power,
Charmer of an idle hour,
Object of my warm desire,
Lip of wax, and eye of fire,
And thy snowy taper waist
With my finger gently braced,
And thy pretty smiling crest
With my little stopper press'd,
And the sweetest bliss of blisses
Breathing from thy balmy kisses,
Happy thrice and thrice again
Happiest he of happy men,
Who, when again the night returns,
When again the cricket's gay,
(Little cricket full of play)
Can afford his tube to feed
With the fragrant Indian weed.
Pleasure for a nose divine
Incense of the God of wine,
Happy thrice and thrice again,
Happiest he of happy men.

ISAAC HAWKINS BROWNE
A Pipe of Tobacco, 1736

III: BEING AND DOING

CONSIDER the lilies of the field, how they grow; they toil not, neither do they spin: and yet I say unto you that even Solomon in all his glory was not arrayed like one of these.

THE GOSPEL ACCORDING TO ST. MATTHEW

A FOUNTAIN breaks out in the wilderness, but that fountain cares not whether any man comes to fetch water or no; a fresh and fit gale blows upon the sea, but it cares not whether the mariners hoist sail or no; a rose blows in your garden, but it calls you not to smell it.

JOHN DONNE

BUSINESS is really more agreeable than pleasure; it interests the whole mind, the aggregate nature of man, more continuously, and more deeply. But it does not *look* as if it did.

WALTER BAGEHOT

THOUGH the most be players, some must be spectators.

BEN JONSON

O LADY, leave thy silken thread
    And flowery tapestrie,
There's living roses on the bush,
    And blossoms on the tree;
Stoop where thou wilt, thy careless hand
    Some random bud will meet;
Thou canst not tread, but thou wilt find
    The daisy at thy feet.

'Tis like the birthday of the world,
    When earth was born in bloom;
The light is made of many dyes,
    The air is all perfume;
There's crimson buds, and white and blue—
    The very rainbow showers
Have turned to blossoms where they fell,
    And sown the earth with flowers.

There's fairy tulips in the East,
    The garden of the sun;
The very streams reflect the hues,
    And blossom as they run:
While morn opes like a crimson rose,
    Still wet with pearly showers;
Then, Lady, leave the silken thread
    Thou twinest into flowers.

THOMAS HOOD, in the *Forget Me Not*, 1825

A CONFLICT

THERE were mornings when, casting off at dawn, I drifted through long cool shadows, watching the sunlight on the trees creep down to meet the water, hearing no sound but the tremolo of the aspens, seeing no one but a chance sportsman and his dog. There were noons with cooling breezes and flocculent clouds high in the sky, and evenings when the forest rang with bird song and the river was a sheet of moving glass. There were nights when, looking skywards, the passing clouds seemed like new continents and islands marked on the inside of a mighty globe.

Hereabouts there was just enough current to keep me moving through the stretches of restful, unexciting landscape. I could relax and let fancies flitter through my brain as inconsequentially as a lady-bird or a drowsy moth might rest a moment on the gunwale.

The trouble with just 'being' is that you get nothing done. The trouble with 'doing' is that it makes you unconscious of 'being'. Nothing is worth doing unless you concentrate your thoughts upon it, yet if you do that you miss the consciousness of the doing, and enjoy only the having done.

ROBERT GIBBINGS
Coming Down the Seine, 1953

A SOLUTION

THE world contains so many beautiful things to gaze at
That gazing is an occupation that you could spend days at,
And these beautiful things are of so many different kinds, or shall
    we say heterogeneous,
Such as the sun and moon etc. and butterflies and mermaids etc.
    that to list them all you would have to be an etcetera genius
So I shall hasten to a landing
And mention two beautiful things that are to my mind outstanding,
And one of them is to be on a train,
And see what we see when we flatten our noses against the pane,
And the other is wistful enough to make anybody feel cosmic and
    pious,
Which is to stand beside the track and wave at the passengers as they
    rocket by us,
So that is why rather than be an etcetera or any other kind of genius
I would rather be schizophrenious,
Because I should regard it as the most satisfactory of stunts
To be able to split my personality and be in two places at once,
For who could be so happy as I
Sitting with my nose against a train window watching me wave to
    me as I go rocketing by?

OGDEN NASH, *Good Intentions*, 1942

BUSYNESS AND IDLENESS

EXTREME busyness, whether at school or college, kirk or market, is a symptom of deficient vitality; and a faculty for idleness implies a catholic appetite and a strong sense of personal identity. There is a sort of dead-alive, hackneyed people about, who are scarcely conscious of living except in the exercise of some conventional occupation . . . they cannot be idle, their nature is not generous enough; and they pass those hours in a sort of coma, what are not dedicated to furious moiling in the gold-mill.

ROBERT LOUIS STEVENSON

I LEAVE this notice on my door
For each accustomed visitor:
'I am gone into the fields
To take what this sweet hour yields;
Reflection, you may come tomorrow,
Sit by the fireside of Sorrow.
You with the unpaid bill, Despair,
You tiresome verse-reciter, Care,
I will pay you in the grave,
Death will listen to your stave.
Expectation too, be off!
Today is for itself enough . . .'

PERCY BYSSHE SHELLEY
Posthumous Poems, 1824

PURPOSE AND PLEASURE

THE greater part of Men make their way with the same instinctiveness, the same unwandering eye from their purposes, the same animal eagerness as the Hawk . . . I go among the Fields and catch a glimpse of a Stoat or a fieldmouse peeping out of the withered grass—the creature hath a purpose, and its eyes are bright with it. I go amongst the buildings of a city and I see a Man hurrying along —to what? The Creature has a purpose, and his eyes are bright with it . . .

JOHN KEATS, Letter, 19 March, 1819

Not he that knows how to acquire,
    But to enjoy, is blessed.
Nor does our happiness consist
    In motion, but in rest.

The gods pass man in bliss, because
    They toil not for more height,
But can enjoy, and in their own
    Eternal rest delight.

Then, princess, do not toil, nor care;
    Enjoy what you possess;
Which whilst you do, you equalize
    The gods in happiness.

THOMAS MAY
The Tragedy of Cleopatra, 1639
(acted 1626)

77

THE MOOD OF MAY

WHEN May is in his prime, then may each heart rejoice:
When May bedecks each branch with green, each bird strains forth
   his voice.
The lively sap creeps up into the blooming thorn;
The flowers, which cold in prison kept, now laugh the frost to scorn.
All nature's imps triumph whiles joyful May doth last;
When May is gone, of all the year the pleasant time is past.

May makes the cheerful hue, May breeds and brings new blood;
May marcheth throughout every limb, May makes the merry
   mood.
May pricketh tender hearts their warbling notes to tune:
Full strange it is, yet some we see do make their May in June.
Thus things are strangely wrought whiles joyful May doth last;
Take May in time, when May is gone the pleasant time is past.

All ye that live on earth, and have your May at will,
Rejoice in May, as I do now, and use your May with skill.
Use May while that you may, for May hath but his time,
When all the fruit is gone, it is too late the tree to climb.
Your liking and your lust is fresh whiles May doth last;
When May is gone, of all the year the pleasant time is past.

RICHARD EDWARDS
The Paradise of Dainty Devices, 1576

BROIDERED PICTURE: ENGLISH, *c.* 1660

ARMILLARY SPHERE: GERMAN, SIXTEENTH CENTURY

Now for my life, it is a miracle of thirty years, which to relate were not a history, but a piece of poetry, and would sound to common ears like a fable; for the world, I count it not an Inn, but an Hospital; and a place not to live, but to die in. The world that I regard is my self; it is the microcosm of my own frame that I cast mine eye on: for the other, I use it but like my Globe, and turn it round sometimes for my recreation. Men that look upon my outside, perusing only my condition and fortunes, do err in my Altitude, for I am above Atlas his shoulders. The earth is a point, not only in respect of the Heavens above us, but of that Heavenly and Celestial part within us: that mass of flesh that circumscribes me, limits not my mind; that surface that tells the Heavens it hath an end, cannot persuade me I have any; I take my circle to be above three hundred and sixty; though the number of the arc do measure my body, it comprehendeth not my mind; whilst I study to find how I am a Microcosm, or little world, I find myself something more than the great. There is surely a piece of Divinity in us; something that was before the elements, and owes no homage unto the Sun. Nature tells me I am the Image of God, as well as Scripture: he that understands not thus much hath not his introduction or first lesson, and is yet to begin the Alphabet of man. I am the happiest man alive: I have that in me that can convert poverty into riches, adversity into prosperity: I am more invulnerable than Achilles; Fortune hath not one place to hit me ... In brief, I am content, and what should Providence add more? Surely this is what we call Happiness, and this do I enjoy: with this I am happy in a dream, and as content to enjoy a happiness in a fancy as others in a more apparent truth and realty.

SIR THOMAS BROWNE, *Religio Medici*, 1642

FROM THE HEIGHTS

WHAT are the feelings of the climber himself? When he reaches the long-desired little stance above the lower portion of the crack he will halt for a few moments, and while thus halted his gaze will stray away from the prospect of his continued labours. He will glance far down the grey slices of precipice into the sunless depths of the long couloir he has ascended to the foot of the crack, and his eyes will seek the Mer de Glace, which appears from above not unlike some monstrous dragon, frozen in the act of wriggling from its lair to devour Chamonix. He will look downwards into violet depths and upwards to shining heights, or peer between fugitive mists that are ever vignetting some new enchantment of form or colour.

These things he will see, while his breast heaves with his previous exertions. Yet, at the time, they are meaningless to him. His thoughts are concentrated upon his position and the problem before him.

But all the time his brain is registering his visions, and months later as he sits by the winter fireside these visions will recur. For a few minutes he will be lost to his surroundings. Once more he will find himself high up on the sunny precipice, remembering not the discomforts, the anxieties, or the physical stresses of the climb, but the beauties and grandeurs that were around him. He will see again the thin-edged spires splintering the blue sky, the silvery blades of wind-carved snow, the stern rock-towers threatening his progression, the lacery and tracery of glaciers at his feet. He will remember the pure joy of conquest unattended by mean rivalry, bloodshed, or the feverish clamour of his fellow-men.

F. S. SMYTHE, *Climbs and Ski Runs*, 1932

TO THE DEPTHS

THE cavern shrank again, the walls almost touched, and the ceiling seemed to join the floor. The remaining passage was a regular cat-hole, and we had to wriggle in in true cat fashion. We bowed one another in as if in a drawing-room; M. Catala was the first to go through, flat on his stomach. He crawled laboriously, while the rest of us waited anxiously with our heads together and our lamps on the ground. His feet disappeared; we heard the rubbing of cloth, the grating of hobnails on the stone, a stifled groan. Finally there was a moment's silence while he stood up and pointed his light ahead. The next sign of life was a roar of astonished triumph; finally we heard him shout through the tunnel: 'The white sea!'

His words recalled one of the most extraordinary scenes in my old favourite, Verne's *Journey to the Centre of the Earth*. I flung myself into the tunnel, and scrambled out at the other end, followed by the rest of the party.

A white, brilliant, coagulated surface spread out under our feet; it was terminated by high cliffs, also white. Nowhere but under-ground could we have seen such a spectacle. This smooth, unbroken expanse was neither water nor ice; it was a floor of moist, shiny stalagmite. The walls were covered with a dull, granular deposit, deceptively like the sides of an ice-floe.

The frozen sea rang under our feet as we walked. The whole thing was so like a polar scene that we thought we felt a chill breeze. So we did, in fact; it was not an illusion. The resemblance was unimaginably perfect. We walked Indian file through an arctic wilderness, and the unreal, diffuse light of our lamps must have been like that of the midnight sun. To cap it all, the stalagmite cracked and gave under my weight, and my leg sank in as I jumped away.

I returned cautiously to the gaping hole; it was full of clear water, of the turquoise cast peculiar to glaciers.

If I had been alone when I saw these marvels, I would hardly dare describe them now for fear of sceptical smiles. But the absolute stupefaction of my companions is a sign that I am not exaggerating. And there were yet more astonishing things to come.

The white sea narrowed to a winding fjord between beetling cliffs; then the surface rose to the foot of a petrified waterfall. Beyond, the gallery continued narrow; its walls were covered with a spiny deposit which hooked and scratched the would-be passer-by. We scrambled up an abrupt rise out of the corridor into a spacious chamber.

Here we stood speechless. Just when we thought we had exhausted our powers of admiration, we stepped into a fairy palace. Hundreds of caverns and countless strange stories and pictures had not prepared me for marvels like these.

Stalactites and crystals sparkled everywhere; their profusion, their whiteness, their shapes were fantastic beyond belief. We were inside a precious stone; it was a palace of crystal. But that is a mere cliché for what we saw. I will not pile up superlatives by attempting a general description. Even in colouring and delicacy the formations surpassed the most gorgeous flowers of nature.

There were microscopic stalactites and flawlessly transparent giant crystals. There were shiny formations, dull formations, smooth formations, spiny formations, milky, red, black, crude green formations. The colours came from mineral infiltrations, of which the mountain has a rich and varied store. Finally, there were two entirely new phenomena, still unexplained: huge needles as fine as cobwebs, which trembled and broke at a breath, and silver strings with the brilliance of silk yarn, which dangled from roof and walls.

NORBERT CASTERET, *Ten Years Under the Earth*, translated by Barrows Mussey, 1939

A CARP IN A POOL:
COLOURED WOODCUT
BY KATSUSHIKA TAITO
NINETEENTH CENTURY

DARK ECSTASIES

In a cool curving world he lies
And ripples with dark ecstasies.
The kind luxurious lapse and steal
Shapes all his universe to feel
And know and be; the clinging stream
Closes his memory, glooms his dream,
Who lips the roots o' the shore, and glides
Superb on unreturning tides.
Those silent waters weave for him
A fluctuant mutable world and dim,
Where wavering masses bulge and gape
Mysterious, and shape to shape
Dies momently through whorl and hollow,
And form and line and solid follow
Solid and line and form to dream
Fantastic down the eternal stream;
An obscure world, a shifting world,
Bulbous, or pulled to thin, or curled,
Or serpentine, or driving arrows,
Or serene slidings, or March narrows.
There slipping wave and shore are one,
And weed and mud. No ray of sun,
But glow to glow fades down the deep
(As dream to unknown dream in sleep);
Shaken translucency illumes
The hyaline of drifting glooms . . .

RUPERT BROOKE, from 'The Fish'
Poems, 1911

STANDING STILL

Broad August burns in milky skies,
    The world is blanched with hazy heat;
The vast green pasture, even, lies
    Too hot and bright for eyes and feet.

Amid the grassy levels rears
    The sycamore against the sun
The dark boughs of a hundred years
    The emerald foliage of one.

Lulled in a dream of shade and sheen
    With the clement twilight thrown,
By that great cloud of floating green
    A horse is standing, still as stone.

He stirs nor head nor hoof, although
    The grass is fresh beneath the branch;
His tail alone swings to and fro
    In graceful curves from haunch to haunch.

He stands quite lost, indifferent
    To rock or pasture, trace or rein;
He feels the vaguely sweet content
    Of perfect sloth in limb and brain.

WILLIAM CANTON, 'Day-Dreams'
A Lost Epic and other Poems, 1887

SITTING AND LOOKING

I KNOW nothing so pleasant as to sit there on a summer afternoon, with the western sun flickering through the great elder-tree, and lighting up our gay parterres, where flowers and flowering shrubs are set as thick as grass in a field, a wilderness of blossoms, interwoven, intertwined, wreathy, garlandy, profuse beyond all profusion, where we may guess that there is such a thing as mould, but never see it. I know nothing so pleasant as to sit in the shade of that dark bower, with the eye resting on that bright piece of colour, lighted so gloriously by the evening sun, now catching a glimpse of the little birds as they fly rapidly in and out of their nests—for there are always two or more birds'-nests in the thick tapestry of cherry-trees, honeysuckle, and china-roses which covers our walls—now tracing the gay gambols of the common butterflies, as they sport around the dahlias; now watching that rarer moth, which the country people, fertile in pretty names, call the bee-bird; that bird-like insect which flutters in the hottest days over the sweetest flowers, inserting its long proboscis into the small tube of the jessamine, and hovering over the scarlet blossoms of the geranium, whose bright colour seems reflected on its own feathery breast; that insect, which seems so thoroughly a creature of the air, never at rest; always, even when feeding, self-poised and self-supported, and whose wings, in their ceaseless motion, have a sound so deep, so full, so lulling, so musical.

Nothing so pleasant as to sit amid that mixture of the flower and the leaf, watching the bee-bird! Nothing so pretty to look at as my garden! It is quite a picture; only unluckily it resembles a picture in more qualities than one,—it is fit for nothing but to look at.

MARY RUSSELL MITFORD, *Our Village*, vol. 3, 1828

ALONE IN A WOOD

IT was still almost summer in the heart of the wood; and as soon as I had scrambled through the hedge, I found myself in a dim green forest atmosphere under eaves of virgin foliage. In places where the wood had itself for a background and the trees were massed together thickly, the colour became intensified and almost gem-like: a perfect fire of green, that seemed none the less green for a few specks of autumn gold. None of the trees were of any considerable age or stature; but they grew well together, I have said; and as the road turned and wound among them, they fell into pleasant groupings and broke the light up pleasantly. Sometimes there would be a colonnade of slim, straight tree-stems with the light running down them as down the shafts of pillars, that looked as if it ought to lead to something, and led only to a corner of sombre and intricate jungle. Sometimes a spray of delicate foliage would by thrown out flat, the light lying flatly along the top of it, so that against a dark background it seemed almost luminous. There was a great hush over the thicket (for indeed, it was more of a thicket than a wood); and the vague rumours that went among the tree-tops, and the occasional rustling of big birds or hares among the undergrowth, had in them a note of almost treacherous stealthiness, that put the imagination on its guard and made me walk warily on the russet carpet of last year's leaves. The spirit of the place seemed to be all attention; the wood listened as I went, and held its breath to number my footfalls.

ROBERT LOUIS STEVENSON, from 'An Autumn Effect'
Essays of Travel, 1905 (written 1875)

PEAMOOR
WATERCOLOUR BY FRANCIS

FÊTE CHAMPÊTRE

THE other evening we happened to be got together in a company of eighteen people, men and women of the best fashion here, at a garden in the town to walk; when one of the ladies bethought herself of asking, 'Why should we not sup here?' Immediately the cloth was laid by the side of a fountain under the trees, and a very elegant supper served up; after which another said, 'Come, let us sing'; and directly began herself. From singing we insensibly fell to dancing, and singing in a round; when somebody mentioned the violins, and immediately a company of them was ordered. Minuets were begun in the open air, and then came country dances, which held till four o'clock next morning, at which hour the gayest lady there proposed that such as were weary should get into their coaches, and the rest of them should dance before them, with the music in the van; and in this manner we paraded through all the principal streets of the city, and waked every body in it.

THOMAS GRAY
Letter to his Mother from Rheims, June 21, 1739

WALKING ALONE

GIVE me the clear blue sky over my head, and the green turf beneath my feet, a winding road before me, and a three hours' march to dinner—and then to thinking! It is hard if I cannot start some game on these lone heaths. I laugh, I run, I leap, I sing for joy. From the point of yonder rolling cloud I plunge into my past being, and revel there, as the sun burnt Indian plunges headlong into the wave that wafts him to his native shore. Then long-forgotten things, like 'sunken wrack and sumless treasuries', burst upon my eager sight, and I begin to feel, think, and be myself again. Instead of an awkward silence broken by attempts at wit or dull commonplaces, mine is that undisturbed silence of the heart which is above perfect eloquence. No one likes puns, alliterations, antithesis, argument, and analysis better than I do; but I sometimes had rather be without them. 'Leave, oh, leave me to my repose!' I have just now other business in hand, which would seem idle to you, but is with me 'very stuff of the conscience'. Is not this wild rose sweet without a comment? Does not this daisy leap to my heart set in its coat of emerald? Yet if I were to explain to you the circumstance that has so endeared it to me, you would only smile. Had I not better then keep it to myself, and let it serve me to brood over, from here to yonder craggy point, and from thence onwards to the far-distant horizon? I should be but bad company all that way, and therefore prefer being alone.

WILLIAM HAZLITT
from 'On Going a Journey', *Table Talk*, 1822

94

RECIPE FOR A PICNIC

PROVIDED care has been taken in choosing congenial guests, and that in a mixed party one sex does not preponderate, a well arranged picnic is one of the pleasantest forms of entertainment.

Watch carefully not to provide too much of one thing and too little of another; avoid serving plenty of salad and no dressing; two or three legs of lamb and no mint sauce; an abundance of wine and no corkscrew; and suchlike little mistakes. Given a happy party of young people bent on enjoyment, these are trifles light as air, which serve rather to increase the fun than diminish it. But, on the other hand, the party may not all be young and merry; it may be very distasteful to some to have to suffer these inconveniences.

The easiest way to arrange that there should be nothing wanting, is to make out a menu, adding all the little etceteras. It is advisable to estimate quantities extravagantly, for nothing is more annoying than to find everything exhausted and guests hungry. Following is a list of articles that should be provided in addition to the repast:

Wines, bottled beer, soda-water, lemonade. Plates, knives, forks, spoons, glasses, tumblers, tablecloths, serviettes, glass cloths, pepper, cayenne, salt, mustard, oil, vinegar, castor sugar, corkscrews, and champagne-opener. A chafing dish and accessories are very useful accompaniments to a picnic.

ISABELLA BEETON
Beeton's Book of Household Management, 1861

95

TAVERN TALK

SOME men's whole delight is to take tobacco, and drink day long
in a tavern or ale-house, to discourse, sing, all jest, roar, talk of a
Cock and a Bull over a pot, &c.

ROBERT BURTON, *The Anatomy of Melancholy*, 1621

WOULD you know how we meet o'er our jolly full bowls?
As we mingle our liquors we mingle our souls:
The sweet melts the sharp, the kind soothes the strong,
And nothing but friendship grows all the night long.
　　We drink, laugh, and gratify every desire
　　Love only remains, our unquenchable fire.

THOMAS OTWAY, in *The Theatre of Music, II*, 1685

I HAVE heard him assert, that a tavern-chair was the throne of human
felicity—'As soon', said he, 'as I enter the door of a tavern, I experience an oblivion of care, and a freedom from solicitude: when I am
seated, I find the master courteous, and the servants obsequious to
my call; anxious to know and ready to supply my wants: wine there
exhilarates my spirits, and prompts me to free conversation and an
interchange of discourse with those whom I most love: I dogmatize
and am contradicted, and in this conflict of opinions and sentiments
I find delight.'

SIR JOHN HAWKINS, *Life of Dr. Johnson*, 1787

POETRY IN PRISON

I NOW write to you from my confinement in Newgate, where I have been ever since Monday last was sennight, and where I enjoy myself with much more tranquillity than I have known for upwards of a twelve-month past; having a room entirely to myself, and pursuing the amusement of my poetical studies, uninterrupted, and agreeable to my mind. I thank the Almighty, I am now all collected in myself; and though my person is in confinement, my mind can expatiate on ample and useful subjects with all the freedom imaginable. I am now more conversant with the Nine than ever; and if instead of a Newgate Bird, I may be allowed to be a Bird of the Muses, I assure you, Sir, I sing very freely in my cage; sometimes indeed in the plaintive notes of the nightingale; but at others in the cheerful strains of the lark.

    RICHARD SAVAGE, Letter to a friend, January 30, 1743
    in Samuel Johnson's *Life of Savage*, 1744

. . . Stone walls do not a prison make,
   Nor iron bars a cage;
Minds innocent and quiet take
   That for an hermitage:
If I have freedom in my love,
   And in my soul am free,
Angels alone, that soar above,
   Enjoy such liberty.

    RICHARD LOVELACE, *Lucasta*, 1649

FOIBLES

LORD BUTE, when young, possessed a very handsome person, of which advantage he was not insensible; and he used to pass many hours every day, as his enemies asserted, occupied in contemplating the symmetry of his own legs.

SIR NATHANIEL WRAXALL, *Historical Memoirs*, 1836

'IF (said he) I had no duties, and no reference to futurity, I would spend my life in driving briskly in a post-chaise with a pretty woman; but she should be one who could understand me, and would add something to the conversation.'

JAMES BOSWELL, *Life of Dr. Johnson*, 1791

... OVER Lamb, at this period of his life, there passed regularly, after taking wine, a brief eclipse of sleep. It descended upon him as softly as a shadow. In a gross person, laden with superfluous flesh, and sleeping heavily, this would have been disagreeable; but in Lamb, thin even to meagreness, spare and wiry as an Arab of the desert, or as Thomas Aquinas, wasted by scholastic vigils, the affection of sleep seemed rather a network of aerial gossamer than of earthly cobweb—more like a golden haze falling upon him gently from the heavens than a cloud exhaling upwards from the flesh. Motionless in his chair as a bust, breathing so gently as scarcely to seem certainly alive, he presented the image of repose midway between life and death, like the repose of sculpture; and, to one who knew his history, a repose affectingly contrasting with the calamities and internal storms of his life.

THOMAS DE QUINCEY, *Leaders in Literature*, 1858

MORE FOIBLES

I MENTIONED that Lord Monboddo told me he awaked every morning at four, and then for his health got up and walked in his room naked, with the window open, which he called taking an air bath; after which he went to bed again, and slept two hours more.

JAMES BOSWELL, *Life of Dr. Johnson*, 1791

AT night, when he was abed, and the doors made fast, and was sure nobody heard him, he sang aloud (not that he had a very good voice) but for his health's sake: he did believe it did his lungs good, and conduced much to prolong his life.

JOHN AUBREY
on Thomas Hobbes, *Brief Lives*, 1813

I LOVE in Isa's bed to lie
O such a joy and luxury
The bottom of the bed I sleep
And with great care I myself keep
Oft I embrace her feet of lillys
But she has goton all the pillies
Her neck I never can embrace
But I do hug her feet in place.

MARJORIE FLEMING, quoted by DR. JOHN
BROWN, *Horae Subsecivae*, 1858

99

ON ICE

>   . . . ALL shod with steel
> We hissed along the polished ice in games . . .
> And not a voice was idle: with the din
> Smitten, the precipices rang aloud;
> The leafless trees and every icy crag
> Tinkled like iron; while far distant hills
> Into the tumult sent an alien sound
> Of melancholy not unnoticed, while the stars
> Eastward were sparkling clear, and in the west
> The orange sky of evening died away.
> Not seldom from the uproar I retired
> Into a silent bay, or sportively
> Glanced sideway, leaving the tumultuous throng,
> To cut across the reflex of a star
> That fled, and, flying still before me, gleamed
> Upon the glassy plain: and oftentimes,
> When we had given our bodies to the wind,
> And all the shadowy banks on either side
> Came sweeping through the darkness, spinning still
> The rapid line of motion, then at once
> Have I, reclining back upon my heels,
> Stopped short; yet still the solitary cliffs
> Wheeled by me—even as if the earth had rolled
> With visible motion her duirnal round!
> Behind me did they stretch in solemn train,
> Feebler and feebler, and I stood and watched
> Till all was tranquil as a dreamless sleep.

WILLIAM WORDSWORTH, *The Prelude,* 1850
(written 1799–1805)

'INTER LANDSCAPE (DETAIL): PAINTING BY PIETER BRUEGHEL 1565

THE MOAT:
PAINTING BY
JOHN NASH
c. 1922

STILL WATERS

I WALK of grey noons by the old canal
   Where rain-drops patter on the autumn leaves
Now watching from some ivied orchard wall
   In slopes of stubble figures pile the sheaves;
Or under banks in shadow of their grass,
Blue water-flies by starts jettingly pass
'Mid large leaves level on the glassy cool;
   Or noiseless dizzy midges winking round
The yellow sallows of the meadow pool;
   While into cloudy silence ebbs each sound,
And sifts the moulting sunlight warm and mellow
   O'er sandy beach remote, or slumberous flood,
   Or rooky, red brick mansion by the wood,
Mossed gate, or farmyard hay-stacks tanned and yellow.

THOMAS CAULFIELD IRWIN
Sonnets on the Poetry and Problems of Life, 1881

ABROAD

EARLY morning on the Mediterranean: bright air resinous with Aleppo pine, water spraying over the gleaming tarmac of the Route Nationale and darkly reflecting the spring-summer green of the planes; swifts wheeling round the oleander, waiters unpiling the wicker chairs and scrubbing the cafe tables; armfuls of carnation on the flower-stall, pyramids of lemon and aubergine, *rascasses* on the fishmonger's slab goggling among the wine-dark urchins; smell of brioches from the bakers, sound of reed curtains jingling in the barber shop, clang of the tin kiosk opening for *Le Petit Var*. Our rope-soles warm up on the cobbles by the harbour where the *Jean D'Agrève* prepares for a trip to the Islands and the Annamese boy scrubs her brass. Now cooks from many yachts step ashore with their market-baskets, one-eyed cats scrounge among the fish-heads, while the hot sun refracts the dancing sea-glitter on the café awning, until the sea becomes a green gin-fizz of stillness in whose depth a quiver of sprats charges and counter-charges in the pleasure of fishes.

PALINURUS, *The Unquiet Grave*, 1945

... IT is an isle 'twixt Heaven, Air, Earth and Sea,
Cradled and hung in clear tranquillity ...
And from the sea there rise, and from the sky
There fall, clear exhalations, soft and bright,
Veil after veil, each hiding some delight,
Which sun or moon or zephyr draw aside,
Till the isle's beauty, like a naked bride
Glowing at once with love and loveliness,
Blushes and trembles at its own excess ...

PERCY BYSSHE SHELLEY, *Epipsychidion*, 1822

AT HOME

Rumbling under blackened girders, Midland, bound for Crickle-
  wood,
Puffed its sulphur to the sunset where that Land of Laundries stood.
Rumble under, thunder over, train and tram alternate go,
Shake the floor and smudge the ledger, Charrington, Sells, Dale
  and Co.,
Nuts and nuggets in the window, trucks along the lines below.

When the Bon Marché was shuttered, when the feet were hot and
  tired,
Outside Charrington's we waited, by the 'STOP HERE IF REQUIRED',
Launched aboard the shopping basket, sat precipitately down,
Rocked past Zwanziger the baker's, and the terrace blackish brown,
And the curious Anglo-Norman parish church of Kentish Town.

Till the tram went over thirty, sighting terminus again,
Past municipal lawn tennis and the bobble-hanging plane;
Soft the light suburban evening caught our ashlar-speckled spire,
Eighteen-sixty Early English, as the mighty elms retire
Either side of Brookfield Mansions flashing fine French-window fire.

Oh the after-tram-ride quiet, when we heard a mile beyond,
Silver music from the bandstand, barking dogs by Highgate Pond;
Up the hill where stucco houses in Virginia creeper drown—
And my childish wave of pity, seeing children carrying down
Sheaves of drooping dandelions to the courts of Kentish Town.

JOHN BETJEMAN, 'Parliament Hill Fields'
New Bats in Old Belfries, 1945

THE CITY IN THE SEA

A CITY of marble, did I say? Nay, rather a golden city, paved with emerald. For truly, every pinnacle and turret glanced or glowed, overlaid with gold, or bossed with jasper. Beneath, the unsullied sea drew in deep breathing, to and fro, its eddies of green wave . . . A wonderful piece of world. Rather, itself a world. It lay along the face of the waters, no larger, as its captains saw it from their masts at evening, than a bar of sunset that could not pass away; but for its power, it must have seemed to them as if they were sailing in the expanse of heaven, and this a great planet, whose orient edge widened through ether. A world from which all ignoble care and petty thoughts were banished, with all the common and poor elements of life. No foulness, nor tumult, in those tremulous streets, that filled, or fell, beneath the moon; but rippled music of majestic change, or thrilling silence. No weak walls could rise above them; no low-roofed cottage, nor straw-built shed. Only the strength as of rock, and the finished setting of stones most precious. And around them, far as the eye could reach, still the soft moving of stainless waters, proudly pure; as not the flower, so neither the thorn nor the thistle, could grow in the glancing fields. Ethereal strength of Alps, dream-like, vanishing in high procession beyond the Torcellan shore; blue islands of Paduan hills, poised in the golden west. Above, free winds and fiery clouds ranging at their will;—brightness out of the north, and balm from the south, and the stars of the evening and morning clear in the limitless light of arched heaven and circling sea.

JOHN RUSKIN, *Modern Painters*, Vol. 5, 1860

...ORGIO MAGGIORE (DETAIL): PAINTING BY FRANCESCO GUARDI

LAMBETH DELFT EARTHENWARE DISH *c.* 1720

A SEAFARER

. . . By many waters and on many ways
I have known golden instants and bright days;
The day on which, beneath an arching sail,
I saw the Cordilleras and gave hail;
The summer day on which in heart's delight
I saw the Swansea Mumbles bursting white;
The glittering day when all the waves wore flags,
And the ship *Wanderer* came with sails in rags;
That curlew-calling time in Irish dusk,
When life became more splendid than its husk,
When the rent chapel on the brae at Slains
Shone with a doorway opening beyond brains;
The dawn when, with a brace-block's creaking cry,
Out of the mist a little barque slipped by,
Spilling the mist with changing gleams of red,
Then gone, with one raised hand and one turned head;
The howling evening when the spindrift's mists
Broke to display the Four Evangelists,
Snow-capped, divinely granite, lashed by breakers,
Wind-beaten bones of long since buried acres;
The night alone near water when I heard
All the sea's spirit spoken by a bird;
The English dusk when I beheld once more
(With eyes so changed) the ship, the citied shore,
The lines of masts, the streets so cheerly trod
(In happier seasons), and gave thanks to God.
All had their beauty, their bright moments' gift,
Their something caught from Time, the ever-swift . . .

JOHN MASEFIELD, from 'Biography'
Philip the King, and other Poems, 1914

A DISCOVERER

To be with Lawrence was a kind of adventure, a voyage of discovery into newness and otherness. For, being himself of a different order, he inhabited a different universe from that of common men—a brighter and intenser world, of which, while he spoke, he would make you free. He looked at things with the eyes, so it seemed, of a man who had been at the brink of death and to whom, as he emerges from the darkness, the world reveals itself as unfathomably beautiful and mysterious. For Lawrence, existence was one continuous convalescence; it was as though he were newly re-born from a mortal illness every day of his life. What these convalescent eyes saw his most casual speech would reveal. A walk with him in the country was a walk through that marvellously rich and significant landscape which is at once the background and the principal personage of all his novels. He seemed to know, by personal experience, what it was like to be a tree or a daisy or a breaking wave or even the mysterious moon itself. He could get inside the skin of an animal and tell you in the most convincing detail how it felt and how, dimly, inhumanly, it thought. Of Black-Eyed Susan, for example, the cow at his New Mexican ranch, he was never tired of speaking, nor was I ever tired of listening to his account of her character and her bovine philosophy.

'He sees', Vernon Lee once said to me, 'more than a human being ought to see. Perhaps,' she added, 'that's why he hates humanity so much.' Why also he loved it so much. And not only humanity: nature too, and even the supernatural. For wherever he looked, he saw more than a human being ought to see; saw more and therefore loved and hated more. To be with him was to find oneself transported to one of the frontiers of human consciousness.

ALDOUS HUXLEY
The Letters of D. H. Lawrence, 1932

TERRA INCOGNITA

HERE in the self is all that man can know
Of Beauty, all the wonder, all the power,
All the unearthly colour, all the glow,
Here in the self which withers like a flower;
Here in the self which fades as hours pass,
And droops and dies and rots and is forgotten
Sooner, by ages, than the mirroring glass
In which it sees its glory still unrotten.
Here in the flesh, within the flesh, behind,
Swift in the blood and throbbing on the bone,
Beauty herself, the universal mind,
Eternal April wandering alone;
The God, the holy Ghost, the atoning Lord,
Here in the flesh, the never yet explored.

JOHN MASEFIELD
Lollingdon Downs and other Poems, 1917

BOOKS

It is not possible to have the true pictures or statues of Cyrus, Alexander, Caesar, no, nor of the kings or great personages of much later years; for the originals cannot last, and the copies cannot but leese of the life and truth. But the images of men's wits and knowledges remain in books, exempted from the wrong of time and capable of perpetual renovation. Neither are they fitly to be called images, because they generate still, and cast their seeds in the minds of others, provoking and causing infinite actions and opinions in succeeding ages: so that, if the invention of the ship was thought so noble, which carrieth riches and commodities from place to place, and consociateth the most remote regions in participation of their fruits, how much more are letters to be magnified, which, as ships, pass through the vast seas of time, and make ages so distant to participate of the wisdom, illuminations and inventions the one of the other?

FRANCIS BACON, *The Advancement of Learning*, 1605

THE ASCENT OF JAMES SADLER AT OXFORD, 1810: AQUATINT BY ROBERT HAVELL

BALLOONS

JOURNEYING on high, the silken castle glides,
Bright as a meteor through the azure tides,
O'er towns, and towers, and temples wins its way,
Or mounts sublime, and gilds the vault of day.
Silent, with upturned eyes, unbreathing crowds
Pursue the floating wonder to the clouds,
And, flushed with transport, or benumbed with fear,
Watch, as it rises, the diminished sphere.
—Now less and less—and now a speck is seen;
And now the fleeting rack obtrudes between . . .
The calm philosopher in ether sails,
Views broader stars, and breathes in purer gales,
Sees, like a map, in many a waving line,
Round Earth's blue plains her lucid waters shine;
Sees at his feet the forky lightnings glow,
And hears innocuous thunders roar below.

ERASMUS DARWIN, *The Loves of the Plants,* 1789

NEW FREEDOM

I HELD the stick forward, nosing down and towards the road to counteract the drift of the wind. It was marvellous. I was aware, because of the nearness of the earth, of the roaring machine, headlong hurtling, racing over the surface of the earth. Sometimes I brought her really very low, and then as I saw trees looming up ahead, lifted her.

At Hilton, I did two turns round the house. I had no eyes for possible members of my family, but only for the elms as I roared off about twice their height.

With the wind behind us on the way back, we were going at the hell of a lick—about 120 miles an hour over the ground, so it was not long before hideous Girton heaved in view. I took her up a bit as I cut across to Chesterton. I shut off and brought her round perfectly to a good landing. 'Time for one more circuit.'

We took off all right, but over the elms the engine missed. Marshall throttled back, took over and lifted her up so steeply that I spoke my thought: 'What are you up to?'

He was gaining height for a conk out. Then he did a right-hand turn, shut the throttle and sang out: 'You've got her'.

I took her in and landed. I was drunk with air. I was wild and driving home sang and shouted, full of realization that we have found a new freedom—a new Ocean. For thousands of years we have crawled or run on the earth, or paddled across the seas, and all the while there has been this great ocean just over our heads in which at last we sail with joy. The longing for the sea: the call of the sea, one has heard of that, and that was the natural adventure in the past. But now it is a longing for the air, to go up. The air is more marvellous than any sea, it holds more beauty, more joy than any Pacific swell or South Sea lagoon.

DAVID GARNETT, *A Rabbit in the Air*, 1932

GOLDEN STAIR

How the blithe lark runs up the golden stair
  That leans through cloudy gates from heaven to earth,
And all alone in the empyreal air
  Fills it with jubilant sweets song of mirth!
    How far he seems, how far
      With the light upon his wings!
    Is it a bird, or star
      That shines, and sings?

What matter if the days be dark and frore,
  That sunbeam tells of other days to be,
And singing in the light that floods him o'er
  In joy he overtakes futurity;
    Under cloud-arches vast
      He peeps, and sees behind
    Great summer coming fast
      Adown the wind.

And now he dives into a rainbow's rivers,
  In streams of gold and purple he is drowned,
Shrilly the arrows of his song he shivers,
  As though the stormy drops were turned to sound;
    And now he issues through,
      He scales a cloudy tower,
    Faintly, like falling dew,
      His fast notes shower . . .

FREDERICK TENNYSON, *Days and Hours*, 1854

AN ENCHANTED GARDEN

I SHALL never forget my surprise and delight on first beholding the bottom of the sea ... The water within the reef was as calm as a pond; and, as there was no wind, it was quite clear, from the surface to the bottom, so that we could see down easily even at a depth of twenty or thirty yards. When Jack and I dived into shallower water, we expected to have found sand and stones, instead of which we found ourselves in what appeared really to be an enchanted garden. The whole of the bottom of the lagoon, as we called the calm water within the reef, was covered with coral of every shape, size and hue. Some portions were formed like large mushrooms; others appeared like the brain of a man, having stalks or necks attached to them; but the most common kind was a species of branching coral, and some portions were of a lovely pale pink colour, others were pure white. Among this there grew large quantities of sea-weed of the richest hues imaginable, and of the most graceful forms; while innumerable fishes —blue, red, yellow, green and striped—sported in and out among the flower-beds of this submarine garden.

R. M. BALLANTYNE, *The Coral Island*, 1860

ANOTHER ENCHANTED GARDEN

I LOVE a still conservatory
    That's full of giant, breathless palms,
Azaleas, clematis and vines,
    Whose quietness great Trees becalms
Filling the air with foliage,
    A curved and dreamy statuary.

I love to hear a cold, pure rill
    Of water trickling low, afar
With sudden little jerks and purls
    Into a tank or stoneware jar,
The song of a tiny sleeping bird
    Held like a shadow in its trill.

I love the mossy quietness
    That grows upon the great stone flags,
The dark tree-ferns, the staghorn ferns,
    The prehistoric, antlered stags
That carven stand and stare among
    The silent, ferny wilderness.

And are they birds or souls that flit
    Among the trees so silently,
And are they fish or ghosts that haunt
    The still pools of the rockery!
For I am but a sculptured rock
    As in that magic place I sit . . .

I watch a white Nyanza float
   Upon a green, untroubled pool,
A fairyland Ophelia, she
   Has cast herself in water cool,
And lies while fairy cymbals ring
   Drowned in her fairy castle moat.

The goldfish sing a winding song
   Below her pale and waxen face,
The water-nymph is dancing by
   Lifting smooth arms with mournful grace,
A stainless white dream she floats on
   While fairies beat a fairy gong.

Silent the Cattleyas blaze
   And thin red orchid shapes of Death
Peer savagely with twisted lips
   Sucking an eerie, phantom breath
With that bright, spotted, fever'd lust
   That watches lonely travellers craze.

Gigantic, mauve and hairy leaves
   Hang like obliterated faces
Full of dim unattained expression
   Such as haunts virgin forest places
When Silence leaps among the trees
   And the echoing heart deceives.

W. J. TURNER
'Magic', *The Hunter*, 1916

UNTHINKING heads, who have not learned to be alone, are in a prison to themselves, if they be not also with others; whereas on the contrary, they whose thoughts are in a fair and hurry within are sometimes fain to retire into company, to be out of the crowd of themselves. He who must needs have company, must needs have sometimes bad company. Be able to be alone. Loose not the advantage of solitude and the society of thy self, nor be only content, but delight to be alone and single with omnipresency. He who is thus prepared, the day is not uneasy nor the night black unto him. Darkness may bound his eyes, not his imagination. In his bed he may lie like Pompey and his sons, in all quarters of the earth, may speculate the universe and enjoy the whole world in the hermitage of himself. Thus the old ascetic Christians found a paradise in a desert, and with little converse on earth held a conversation in heaven; thus they astronomized in caves, and, though they beheld not the stars, had the glory of heaven before them.

SIR THOMAS BROWNE, *Christian Morals,* 1716

DANSONS LA GIGUE!

DANSONS la gigue!

J'aimais surtout ses jolis yeux,
Plus clairs que l'étoile des cieux,
J'aimais ses yeux malicieux.

Dansons la gigue!

Elle avait des façons vraiment
De désoler un pauvre amant,
Que c'en était vraiment charmant!

Dansons la gigue!

Mais je trouve encore meilleur
Le baiser de sa bouche en fleur,
Depuis qu'elle est morte à mon coeur.

Dansons la gigue!

Je me souviens, je me souviens
Des heures et des entretiens,
Et c'est le meilleur de mes biens.

Dansons la gigue!

PAUL VERLAINE, 'Streets'
Romances sans Paroles, 1874

LA DANSE:
YON DRAWING
BY RENOIR
1883

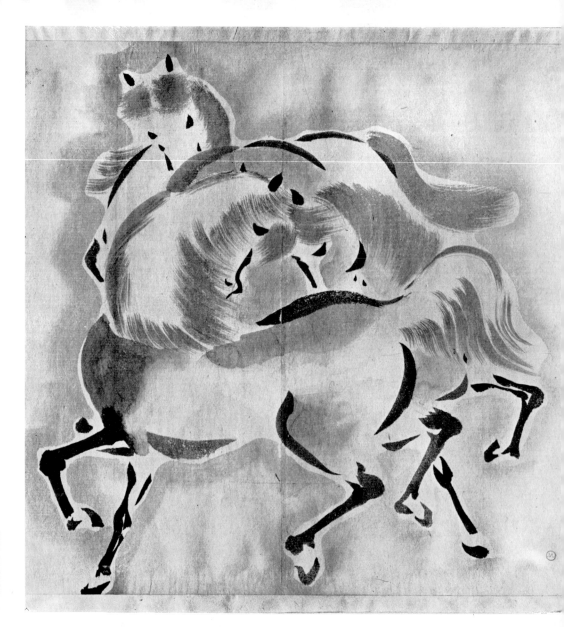

HORSES: JAPANESE DRAWING, NINETEENTH CENTURY

DUMB DELIGHTS

I THINK I could turn and live with animals, they're so placid and
    self-contained:
I stand and look at them long and long.
They do not sweat and whine about their condition;
They do not lie awake in the dark and weep for their sins;
They do not make me sick discussing their duty to God;
Not one is dissatisfied—not one is demented with the mania of
    owning things;
Not one kneels to another, nor to his kind that lived thousands of
    years ago;
Not one is respectable or industrious over the whole earth.

WALT WHITMAN, *Leaves of Grass*, 1881
(written 1855)

THESE exquisite and absurd fancies of mine—little curiosities, and
greedinesses, and impulses to kiss and touch and snatch, and all the
vanities and artless desires that nest and sing in my heart like birds
in a bush—all these, we are now told, are an inheritance from our
pre-human past, and were hatched long ago in very ancient swamps
and forests. But what of that? I like to share in the dumb delights
of birds and animals, to feel my life drawing its sap from roots deep
in the soil of Nature. I am proud of those bright-eyed, furry, four-
footed or scaly progenitors, and not at all ashamed of my cousins,
the Apes and Peacocks and streaked Tigers.

LOGAN PEARSALL SMITH, *Trivia*, 1918

ANIMAL, VEGETABLE

In youth the animal world obsessed me; I saw life through creatures which were in a state of grace, creatures without remorse, without duties, without a past or a future, owning nothing but the intense present and their eternal rhythm of hunger, sleep and play. The ring-tailed lemurs with their reverence for the sun, their leaps through the air and their howls of loneliness, were dark Immortals of a primitive race; the ferrets with their passionate blood-thirst and their tunnelling mania; the beautiful mute genette, the pine-marten, the racoons, the pitiful coati, the dying ocelot, the slow loris—even the animals which I never owned, the beaver, otter, palm-civet and linsang—these bright-fanged, saffron-throated aristocrats held the secret of life for me; they were clues to an existence without thought, guilt or ugliness wherein all was grace, appetite and immediate sensation: Impressionist masterpieces which Nature flung upon the canvas of a day.

Now I care only for the Vegetable world; my day-dreams are no longer of otter-pool and sunny lemurarium, but of slobbering melon, downy quince and dew-dusted nectarine. I feel fruit trees to be an even stranger form of life and therefore more rewarding. Nothing is so alien, so unexpected in a tree as its fruit and yet by the fruit it is known; leaves, height and blossom are sacrificed; so by thinking, reading and maintaining an inner calm we too mature and ripen until the life which once flowered in such careless profusion is concentrated into husks, husks that, like pomegranates or the tomato on our window-sill, continue to mellow long after the leaf has fallen and the plant that bore them rotted to the ground.

PALINURUS, *The Unquiet Grave*, 1945

SPIRITUAL

OFT when my spirit doth spread her bolder wings,
  In mind to mount up to the purest sky,
It down is weighed with thought of earthly things
  And clogged with burden of mortality,
  Where when that sovereign beauty it doth spy,
Resembling heaven's glory in her light,
  Drawn with sweet pleasure's bait, it back doth fly,
And unto heaven forgets her former flight.
There my frail fancy, fed with full delight,
  Doth bathe in bliss and mantleth most at ease:
Me thinks of other heaven, but how it might
    Her heart's desire with most contentment please
    Heart need not with none other happiness,
    But here on earth to have such heaven's bliss.

EDMUND SPENSER
Amoretti and Epithalamion, 1595

LET thy thoughts be of things which have not entered into the hearts of beasts; think of things long past, and long to come; acquaint thyself with the *Choragium* of the stars, and consider the vast expansion beyond them. Let intellectual tubes give thee a glance of things which visive organs reach not. Have a glimpse of incomprehensibles, and thoughts of things which thoughts but tenderly touch. Lodge immaterials in thy head; ascend unto invisibles.

SIR THOMAS BROWNE, *Christian Morals,* 1716

IV : LOVING

THE streets seemed paved with golden stones,
   The boys and girls all mine;
To me how did their lovely faces shine!
   The sons of men all holy ones,
In joy and beauty, then appeared to me;
   And every thing I found
(While like an angel I did see)
   Adorned the ground.

Rich diamonds, and pearl, and gold
   Might everywhere be seen;
Rare colours, yellow, blue, red, white and green,
   Mine eyes on every side behold:
All that I saw, a wonder did appear,
   Amazement was my bliss:
That and my wealth met everywhere:
   No joy to this!

THOMAS TRAHERNE, *Poems of Felicity*, 1903
(written *c.* 1670)

DETAIL FROM THE ANNUNCIATION: PAINTING BY CARLO CRIVELLI, 1486

THE HON.
MRS GRAHAM
PAINTING
BY THOMAS
GAINSBOROU
c. 1777

WOMAN

I CONSIDER woman as a beautiful romantic animal, that may be adorned with furs and feathers, pearls and diamonds, ores and silks. The lynx shall cast its skin at her feet to make her a tippet; the peacock, parrot and swan shall pay contributions to her muff; the sea shall be searched for shells, and the rocks for gems; and every part of nature furnish out its share towards the embellishment of a creature that is the most consummate work of it.

JOSEPH ADDISON, in *The Tatler*, No. 116, 1711

WOMAN (doubtful theme) I sing,
Dear, delightful, dangerous thing!
Magic source of all our joy,
Tempting, trifling, tinselled toy:
Every faculty possessing
That constitutes a curse or blessing:
Witty, empty, fond, capricious,
Pious sometimes, often vicious:
As angels handsome, devils proud,
Modest, pert, submissive, loud:
The most ambiguous work of Heaven,
To cheer us, and torment us, given:
Without them, what, ye gods, is life?
And with them—what but care and strife?

ANONYMOUS, in
A Collection of English Songs, 1796

MAN

My beloved is white and ruddy, the chiefest among ten thousand.
His head is as the most fine gold, his locks are bushy and black as a
raven. His eyes are as the eyes of doves by the rivers of waters,
washed with milk and fitly set. His cheeks are as a bed of spices, as
sweet flowers. His lips like lilies dropping sweet-smelling myrrh.
His hands are as gold rings set with the beryl: his belly is as bright
ivory overlaid with sapphires. His legs are as pillars of marble set
upon sockets of fine gold; his countenance is as Lebanon, excellent
as the cedars. His mouth is most sweet; yea, he is altogether lovely.

Solomon's Song, 10

Lo! in the palace, lo! in the street,
    Beautiful beyond measure;
Yea, gods for glory, and women for sweet,
    The youths, the princes of pleasure!

Idle and crowned in the long day's sun,
    Turbulent, passionate, sad;
Full of the soul of the deed to be done,
    Or the thought of the joy latest had;
They walk their way through the crowds that run,
    They pass through the crowds that part;
And the women behold them, and each knows one,
    How mighty he is in her heart . . .

They win with the vehemence of their souls,
  With the swiftness of their fame;
Their strong and radiant look controls,
  And smiles the world to shame.
Their rule is large, and like fair lords,
  They lavish a goodly treasure;
They live of the joy the world affords
  And they pay the world with pleasure.

One passes bright through the street down there,
  Named and known of repute;
And one hath a scandal of rich flowing hair,
  And the musical tongue of a lute.
O the women, beholding, who thrill and say,
  'While that one stays on the earth,
I can have in the secret of night or of day,
  More delight than a man's life is worth'.

O the woman that says in the midst of the crowd,
  'Beautiful, turbulent one,
Do I not know you through semblance and shroud,
  Even as I know the sun?
Burning, and swift, and divine you are;
  But I have you all to treasure;
Women may love you, but mine you are,
  And prince of the princes of pleasure.'

ARTHUR O'SHAUGHNESSY, from 'A Song of
the Youths', *Music and Moonlight*, 1874

IN LOVE

ONCE did my thoughts both ebb and flow,
  As passion did them move;
Once did I hope, straight fear again—
  And then I was in love.

Once did I waking spend the night,
  And tell how many minutes move;
Once did I wishing waste the day—
  And then I was in love.

Once, by my carving true love's knots,
  The weeping trees did prove
That wounds and tears were both our lots—
  And then I was in love.

Once did I breathe another's breath
  And in my mistress move;
Once was I not mine own at all—
  And then I was in love . . .

Once did I sonnet to my saint,
  My soul in number moved,
Once did I tell a thousand lies—
  And then in truth I loved.

Once in my ear did dangling hang
  A little turtle-dove,
Once, in a word, I was a fool—
  And then I was in love.

ANONYMOUS, set to music by Robert Jones
in *The Muses Garden for Delights*, 1610

POET IN THE CHARACTER OF A SHEPHERD: PAINTING BY SIR PETER LELY, c. 1645

CUPID AND PSYCHE: SCULPTURE IN MARBLE BY CLAUDE AUGUSTIN CAYOT 1706

COME HITHER

COME hither, you that love, and hear me sing
    Of joys still growing,
Green, fresh, and lusty as the pride of spring,
    And ever blowing.
Come hither, youths that blush, and dare not know
    What is desire:
And old men, worse than you, that cannot blow
    One spark of fire;
And with the power of my enchanting song,
Boys shall be able men, and old men young.

Come hither, you that hope, and you that cry;
    Leave off complaining;
Youth, strength, and beauty, that shall never die,
    Are here remaining.
Come hither, fools, and blush you stay so long
    From being blest;
And mad men, worse than you, that suffer wrong,
    Yet seek no rest;
And in an hour, with my enchanting song,
You shall be ever pleased, and young maids long.

JOHN FLETCHER, *The Captain*, 1647

QUESTIONS

WHEN wert thou born, Desire?
   In pride and pomp of May.
By whom, sweet boy, wert thou begot?
   By Self Conceit, men say.
Tell me, who was thy nurse?
   Fresh Youth in sugared joy.
What was thy meat and daily food?
   Sad sighs and great annoy.
What hadst thou then to drink?
   Unfeignëd lovers' tears.
What cradle wert thou rocked in?
   In hope devoid of fears.
What brought thee to thy sleep?
   Sweet thoughts, which liked me best.
And where is now thy dwelling-place?
   In gentle hearts I rest.
Doth company displease?
   It doth, in many one.
Where would Desire then choose to be?
   He loves to muse alone.
What feedeth most thy sight?
   To gaze on favour still.
Whom find'st thou most thy foe?
   Disdain of my good will.
Will ever age or death
   Bring thee unto decay?
No, no! Desire both lives and dies
   A thousand times a day.

EDWARD DE VERE, EARL OF OXFORD, Bodley MS.

AND ANSWERS

Ask me no more where Jove bestows,
When June is past, the fading rose;
For in your beauties, orient deep,
These flowers, as in their causes, sleep.

Ask me no more whither do stray
The golden atoms of the day;
For in pure love heaven did prepare
Those powders to enrich your hair.

Ask me no more whither doth haste
The nightingale, when May is past;
For in your sweet dividing throat
She winters, and keeps warm her note.

Ask me no more where those stars light
That downwards fall in dead of night;
For in your eyes they sit, and there
Fixèd become, as in their sphere.

Ask me no more if east or west
The phoenix builds her spicy nest;
For unto you at last she flies,
And in your fragrant bosom dies.

THOMAS CAREW, *Poems*, 1640

THE NATURE OF LOVE

THAT violence wherewith sometimes a man doteth upon one creature is but a little spark of that love, even towards all, which lurketh in his nature. We are made to love, both to satisfy the necessity of our active nature, and to answer the beauties in every creature. By Love our Souls are married and solder'd to the creatures: and it is our duty like God to be united to them all. We must love them infinitely, but in God, and for God: and God in them: namely all His excellencies manifested in them. When we dote upon the perfections and beauties of some one creature, we do not love that too much, but other things too little. Never was anything in this world loved too much, but many things have been loved in a false way: and all in too short a measure.

THOMAS TRAHERNE, *Centuries of Meditations*, 1908 (written *c.* 1670)

WHAT thing is love? for sure love is a thing.
It is a prick, it is a sting,
It is a pretty, pretty thing;
It is a fire, it is a coal,
Whose flame creeps in at every hole;
And, as my wit doth best devise,
Love's dwelling is in ladies' eyes,
From whence do glance love's piercing darts
That make such holes into our hearts . . .

GEORGE PEELE
The Hunting of Cupid, 1591

MEDICINE FOR LOVE

LOVE, sweet Chloe, is a god, a young youth, and very fair, and winged to fly. And therefore he delights in youth, follows beauty, and gives our phantasy her wings. His power's so vast that that of Jove is not so great. He governs in the elements, rules in the stars, and domineers even o'er the gods that are his peers . . . All flowers are the works of Love. Those plants are his creations, and poems. By him it is that the rivers flow, and by him the winds blow. I have known a bull that has been in love and run bellowing through the meadows as if he had been pricked with a goad; a he-goat, too, so in love with a virgin-she that he has followed her up and down, through the woods, through the lawns. And I myself, when I was young, was in love with Amaryllis, and forgot to eat my meat and drink my drink, and for many tedious nights never could compose to sleep. My panting heart was very sad and anxious, and my body shook with cold: I cried out oft as if I had been thwacked and basted back and sides: and then again was still and mute as if I had lain among the dead. I cast myself into the rivers, as if I had been all on a fire: I called on Pan that he would help me, as having sometimes been himself catched with the love of the peevish Pities. I praised the Echo, that with kindness it restored and trebled to me the dear name of Amaryllis. I broke my pipes, because they could delight, and led the sturdy herds which way I would, and could not draw the forward girl. For there is no medicine for love, neither meat, nor drink, nor any charm, but only kissing and embracing, and lying naked together.

LONGUS, *Daphne and Chloe*
translated by George Thornley, 1657

If the heart of a man is de-press'd with cares, The mist is dis-pell'd when a

wo-man ap-pears; Like the notes of a fid-dle, she sweet-ly, sweet-ly

Rais-es the spir-its, and charms our ears, Ros—es and lil——ies her

cheeks dis—close,   But her ripe lips are more sweet than those.

Press her, Ca-ress her, With blisses, Her kisses Dis-solve us in pleasure and soft re-pose.

AIR TRADITIONAL   WORDS BY JOHN GAY, *The Beggar's Opera*, 1728

PORTRAIT IN A MIRROR

HER shadow with such curious art does gild
The shining mirror, with a new light filled,
That well may she with just amazement eye
What only can pretend with her to vye.
Her other self, like her, surprised does show,
Her features mocks, and mocks her wonder too.
The amorous glance, in striving to excel,
Does seem to court her ever here to dwell;
Proud of the transient shape it does present,
Could gladly wish it fixed and permanent,
Fixed as those statues we in gardens place,
Viewing in fountains still their carvëd face.

    Could it, alas, her portrait but retain,
It would endure no other figure's stain;
What her stamp seals, as sacred to her smile,
No soiling look profanely would defile;
Or should there any beauties be, that dare
Their spots, or graces, by this glass compare,
Her eyes, before theirs, thus it would prefer,
In flattering them by truly showing her . . .

    She, dressing by her glass, her glass has dressed,
And richly with her airy shape possessed.
But when, too soon, the fair unkind retires,
The short-lived beauty that shined there expires . . .
The brittle glass, all darkened thus, will mourn
The frail glory lost, it did return,
And of her radiant likeness then complain
That, naked as it was, 'tis left again.

RICHARD LEIGH, *Poems*, 1675

144

THE TOILET OF VENUS: PAINTING BY SIR PETER PAUL RUBENS

LUCY EBBERTON: PAINTING BY GEORGE KNAPTON

GATHER YE ROSEBUDS

GATHER ye rose-buds while ye may,
   Old Time is still a-flying:
And this same flower that smiles today,
   Tomorrow will be dying.

The glorious lamp of heaven, the sun
   The higher he's a-getting,
The sooner will his race be run,
   And nearer he's to setting.

That age is best which is the first,
   When youth and blood are warmer;
But being spent, the worse, and worst
   Times still succeed the former.

Then be not coy, but use your time;
   And while ye may, go marry:
For having lost but once your prime,
   You may for ever tarry.

ROBERT HERRICK, *Hesperides*, 1648

THE FOUNTAINS SMOKE

THE fountains smoke, and yet no flames they show;
  Stars shine all night, though undiscerned by day;
And trees do spring, yet are not seen to grow;
  And shadows move, although they seem to stay.
    In winter's woe is buried summer's bliss,
    And Love loves most where Love most secret is.

The stillest streams descry the greatest deep;
  The clearest sky is subject to a shower;
Conceit's most sweet whenas it seems to sleep;
  And fairest days do in the morning lower.
    The silent grove sweet nymphs they cannot miss,
    For Love loves most where Love most secret is.

The rarest jewels hidden virtue yield;
  The sweet of traffic is a secret gain;
The year once old doth show a barren field;
  And plants seem dead, and yet they spring again:
    Cupid is blind: the reason why is this:
    Love loveth most where Love most secret is.

ANONYMOUS, set to music by Robert Jones in
The Muse's Garden for Delights, 1610

DEATH OF A HERO

WHAT shall I do to show how much I love her?
   How many millions of sighs can suffice?
That which wins other hearts, never can move her,
   Those common methods of love she'll despise.

I will love more than man e'er loved before me,
   Gaze on her all the day, melt all the night,
Till for her own sake at last she'll implore me
   To love her less, to preserve our delight.

Since gods themselves could not ever be loving,
   Men must have breathing recruits for new joys;
I wish my love could be always improving,
   Though eager love, more than sorrow, destroys.

In fair Aurelia's arms leave me expiring
   To be embalmed by the sweets of her breath,
To the last moment I'll still be desiring:
   Never had hero so glorious a death.

THOMAS BETTERTON, *The Prophetess*, 1690

THE WINGED CHARIOT

HAD we but world enough, and time,
This coyness, lady, were no crime,
We would sit down, and think which way
To walk, and pass our long love's day.
Thou by the Indian Ganges' side
Shouldst rubies find: I by the tide
Of Humber would complain. I would
Love you ten years before the flood,
And you should, if you please, refuse
Till the conversion of the Jews;
My vegetable love should grow
Vaster than empires and more slow;
An hundred years should go to praise
Thine eyes, and on thy forehead gaze;
Two hundred to adore each breast,
But thirty thousand to the rest;
An age at least to every part,
And the last age should show your heart.
For, lady, you deserve this state,
Nor would I love at lower rate,
    But at my back I always hear
Time's wingèd chariot hurrying near,
And yonder all before us lie
Deserts of vast eternity . . .

ANDREW MARVELL, *Miscellaneous Poems,* 1684
(written before 1653)

WATCH BY EDWARD EAST IN ENAMELLED GOLD CASE: MID-SEVENTEENTH CENTURY

WHEN BEAUTY AND BEAUTY MEET

WHEN Beauty and Beauty meet
  All naked, fair to fair,
The earth is crying-sweet,
  And scattering-bright the air,
Eddying, dizzying, closing round
  With soft and drunken laughter;
Veiling all that may befall
  After—after—

Where Beauty and Beauty met,
  Earth's still a-tremble there,
And winds are scented yet,
  And memory-soft the air,
Bosoming, folding glints of light,
  And shreds of shadowy laughter;
Not the tears that fill the years
  After—after—

RUPERT BROOKE
1914 and other Poems, 1915

ARITHMETIC OF THE LIPS

GIVE me a kiss from those sweet lips of thine
And make it double by enjoining mine,
Another yet, nay yet and yet another,
And let the first kiss be the second's brother.
Give me a thousand kisses and yet more;
And then repeat those that have gone before;
Let us begin while daylight springs in heaven,
And kiss till night descends into the even,
And when that modest secretary, night,
Discolours all but thy heaven beaming bright,
We will begin revels of hidden love
In that sweet orb where silent pleasures move.
In high new strains, unspeakable delight,
We'll vent the dull hours of the silent night:
Were the bright day no more to visit us,
Oh, then for ever would I hold thee thus,
Naked, enchained, empty of idle fear,
As the first lovers in the garden were.
I'll die betwixt thy breasts that are so white,
For, to die there, would do a man delight.
Embrace me still, for time runs on before,
And being dead we shall embrace no more.
Let us kiss faster than the hours do fly,
Long live each kiss and never know to die . . .
Let us vie kisses, till our eyelids cover,
And if I sleep, count me an idle lover;
Admit I sleep, I'll still pursue the theme,
And eagerly I'll kiss thee in a dream . . .

ANONYMOUS, in *Wit's Recreations*, 1641

154

THE MEANING OF A KISS

. . . ALTHOUGH the mouth be a parcel of the body, yet is it an issue for the words, that be the interpreters of the soul, and for the inward breath, which is also called the soul. And therefore hath a delight to join his mouth with a woman's beloved with a kiss: not to stir him to any dishonest desire, but because he feeleth that that bond is the opening of an entry to the souls, which, drawn with a coveting the one of the other, pour themselves by turn the one into the other body, and be so mingled together that each of them hath two souls.

BALDASSARE CASTIGLIONE, *The Courtier*
translated by Sir Thomas Hoby, 1561

All the breath and the bloom of the year in the bag of one bee:
All the wonder and wealth of the mine in the heart of one gem:
In the core of one pearl all the shade and the shine of the sea:
Breath and bloom, shade and shine,—wonder, wealth, and—how far
    above them—
      Truth, that's brighter than gem,
      Trust, that's purer than pearl—
Brightest truth, purest trust in the universe—
      All were for me in the kiss of one girl.

ROBERT BROWNING, 'Summum Bonum', *Asolando*, 1889

LOVE'S TOY

FOR various purpose serves the Fan,
   As thus—a decent blind,
Between the sticks to peep at man,
   Nor yet betray your mind.

Each action has a meaning plain:
   Resentment's in the snap;
A flirt expresses strong disdain,
   Consent—a tiny tap.

All passions will the Fan disclose,
   All modes of female art;
And to advantage sweetly shows
   The hand—if not the heart.

'Tis Folly's sceptre, first designed
   By love's capricious Boy,
Who knows how lightly all mankind
   Are governed by a toy.

ROBERT LLOYD, *The Capricious Lovers*, 1764

EIGHTEENTH-CENTURY
PHOTOGRAPH BY EDWIN

EMBROIDERED CUSHION: ENGLISH, MID-SEVENTEENTH CENTURY

LOVE IN A GARDEN

AND now what monarch would not gardener be,
My fair Amanda's stately gait to see?
How her feet tempt! how soft and light she treads,
Fearing to wake the flowers from their beds!
Yet from their sweet green pillows everywhere,
They start and gaze about to see my Fair.
Look at yon flower yonder, how it grows
Sensibly! how it opes its leaves and blows,
Puts its best Easter clothes on, neat and gay:
Amanda's presence makes it holiday!
Look how on tiptoe that fair lily stands
To look on thee, and court thy whiter hands
To gather it! I saw in yonder crowd—
That tulip bed of which Dame Flora's proud—
A short dwarf flower did enlarge its stalk,
And shoot an inch to see Amanda walk.
Nay, look, my Fairest! look how fast they grow
Into a scaffold-method spring, as though,
Riding to Parliament, were to be seen
In pomp and state some royal amorous Queen!
The gravelled walks, though even as a die,
Lest some loose pebble should offensive lie,
Quilt themselves o'er with downy moss for thee;
The walls are hanged with blossomed tapestry
To hide their nakedness when looked upon;
The maiden fig tree puts Eve's apron on;
The broad-leaved sycamore, and every tree,
Shakes like the trembling asp, and bends to thee,

And each leaf proudly strives, with fresher air
To fan the curlëd tresses of thy hair.
Nay, and the bee too, with his wealthy thigh,
Mistakes his hive, and to thy lips doth fly,
Willing to treasure up his honey there,
Where honey-combs so sweet and plenty are.
Look how that pretty modest columbine
Hangs down its head, to view those feet of thine!
See the fond motion of the strawberry,
Creeping on th' earth, to go along with thee!
The lovely violet makes after too,
Unwilling yet, my dear, to part with you;
The knot-grass and the daisies catch thy toes,
To kiss my fair one's feet before she goes;
All court and wish me lay Amanda down,
And give my dear a new green-flowered gown.
  Come, let me kiss thee falling, kiss at rise,
  Thou in the garden, I in Paradise.

NATHANIEL HOOKES, *Amanda*, 1653

SAY, crimson rose and dainty daffodil,
    With violet blue,
Since you have seen the beauty of my saint,
    And eke her view,
Did not her sight (fair sight!) you lovely fill
    With sweet delight
Of goddess' grace and angel's sacred taint
    In fine, most bright?

Say, golden primrose, sanguine cowslip fair,
    With pink most fine,
Since you beheld the visage of my dear,
    And eyes divine,
Did not her globy front and glistering hair,
    With cheeks most sweet,
So gloriously like damask flowers appear,
    The gods to greet?

Say, snow-white lily, speckled gilly-flower,
    With daisy gay,
Since you have viewed the queen of my desire
    In brave array,
Did not her ivory paps, fair Venus' bower,
    With heavenly glee,
Of Juno's grace, conjure you to require
    Her face to see?

Say rose, say daffodil, and violet blue,
    With primrose fair,
Since you have seen my nymph's sweet dainty face
    And gesture rare,
Did not (bright cowslip, bloomy pink) her view
    (White lily) shine
(Ah, gilly-flowers and daisy!) with a grace
    Like stars divine?

JOHN REYNOLDS, *The Flower of Fidelity*, 1650

Andantino

I will give my love an ap—ple with—
My head is the ap—ple with—

out e'er a core, I will give my love a house with—
out e'er a core, My mind is the house with—

out e'er a door, I will give my love a pal—ace where—
out e'er a door, My heart is the pal—ace where—

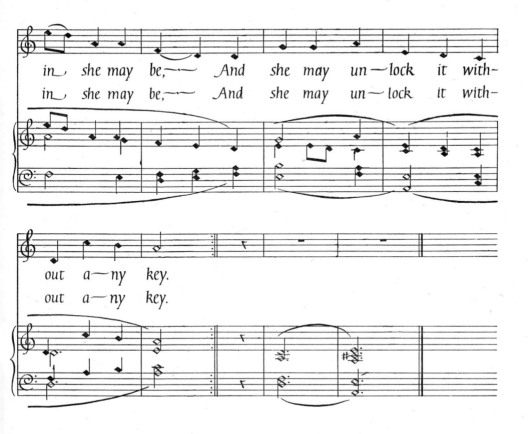

in, she may be,— And she may un—lock it within, she may be,— And she may un—lock it with-

out a—ny key.
out a—ny key.

WORDS AND AIR TRADITIONAL   SETTING BY RALPH VAUGHAN WILLIAMS

I AM half distracted, captain *Shandy*, said Mrs. *Wadman*, holding up
her cambrick handkerchief to her left eye, as she approach'd the door
of my uncle *Toby's* sentry-box—a mote—or sand—or something—
I know not what, has got into this eye of mine—do look into it—it
is not in the white—

In saying which, Mrs. *Wadman* edged herself close in beside my
uncle *Toby*, and squeezing herself down upon the corner of his
bench, she gave him an opportunity of doing it without rising up—
Do look into it—said she.

Honest soul! thou didst look into it with as much innocency of
heart, as ever child look'd into a raree-shew-box; and 'twere as much
a sin to have hurt thee.

If a man will be peeping of his own accord into things of that
nature—I've nothing to say to it—

My uncle *Toby* never did: and I will answer for him, that he would
have sat quietly upon a sofa from *June* to *January* (which, you know,
takes in both the hot and cold months), with an eye as fine as the
Thracian Rodope's beside him, without being able to tell, whether it
was a black or a blue one.

The difficulty was to get my uncle *Toby* to look at one at all.

'Tis surmounted. And

I see him yonder with his pipe pendulous in his hand, and the
ashes falling out of it—looking—and looking—then rubbing his eyes
—and looking again, with twice the good-nature that ever *Galileo*
look'd for a spot in the sun.

In vain! for by all the powers which animate the organ—Widow
Wadman's left eye shines this moment as lucid as her right—there is
neither mote, or sand, or dust, or chaff, or speck, or particle of opake
matter floating in it. There is nothing, my dear paternal uncle! but

one lambent delicious fire, furtively shooting out from every part of it, in all directions, into thine—

If thou lookest, uncle *Toby*, in search of this mote one moment longer—thou art undone . . .

I protest, Madam, said my uncle *Toby*, I see nothing whatever in your eye.

It is not in the white; said Mrs. *Wadman*: my uncle *Toby* look'd with might and main into the pupil—

Now of all the eyes which ever were created—from your own, Madam, up to those of *Venus* herself, which certainly were as venereal a pair of eyes as ever stood in a head—there never was an eye of them all, so fitted to rob my uncle *Toby* of his repose, as the very eye, at which he was looking—it was not, Madam, a rolling eye—a romping or a wanton one—nor was it an eye sparkling— petulant or imperious—of high claims and terrifying exactions, which would have curdled at one that milk of human nature, of which my uncle *Toby* was made up—but 'twas an eye full of gentle salutations—and soft responses—speaking—not like the trumpet stop of some ill-made organ, in which many an eye I talk to, holds coarse converse—but whispering soft—like the last low accent of an expiring saint—'How can you live comfortless, captain *Shandy*, and alone, without a bosom to lean your head on—or trust your cares to?'

It was an eye—

But I shall be in love with it myself, if I say another word about it. It did my uncle *Toby's* business.

LAURENCE STERNE, *Tristram Shandy*, Book VIII, 1765

GOLDEN FETTERS

Whilst I behold thy glittering golden hairs
Dishevelled thus, waving about thy ears,
And see those locks thus loosëd and undone
For their more pomp to sport them in the sun,
Love takes those threads and weaves them with that art
He knits a thousand knots about my heart,
And with such skill and cunning he them sets,
My soul lies taken in those lovely nets,
Making me cry, 'Fair prison, that dost hold
My heart in fetters wrought of burnished gold.'

JAMES MABBE, *Exemplary Novels*, 1640

ECSTASY

WHERE, like a pillow on a bed,
    A pregnant bank swelled up, to rest
The violet's reclining head,
    Sat we two, one another's best.
Our hands were firmly cimented
    With a fast balm, which thence did spring,
Our eye-beams twisted, and did thread
    Our eyes, upon one double string;
So to entergraft our hands, as yet
    Was all the means to make us one,
And pictures in our eyes to get
    Was all our propagation.
As, 'twixt two equal armies, Fate
    Suspends uncertain victory,
Our souls, which to advance their state,
    Were gone out, hung 'twixt her and me.
And whilst our souls negotiate there,
    We like sepulchral statues lay;
All day the same our postures were,
    And we said nothing all the day . . .

JOHN DONNE, from 'The Ecstasy'
Songs and Sonnets, 1633 (written *c.* 1600)

MIRRORS OF LOVE

DEAR, let us two each other spy:
How curious! In each other's eye
We're drawn to life, and thus we see
Ourselves at once, both thee and me,
Distinctly two, yet not alone,
Incorporated, that's but one.

My picture in your eyes you bear:
I yours, as much as mine you wear.
'Tis not our spreties can not pass,
Or shining makes a looking glass,
Nor picture, really we lie
Contracted each in other's eye.

When that our milk-white purer lawn,
Our eyelid curtains, when they're drawn,
Soft sleep, made with sweet vapours' rain,
To cool us shrinks into each brain,
Rejoicing with love's running streams,
Which grosser lovers call but dreams.

Because we two must never part,
We move down to each other's heart,
And there, all passions turned to joy,
Our loving hearts feel no annoy
Delated, lest our souls outskips
With joy, kiss quickly! stop our lips!

WILLIAM CAVENDISH, DUKE OF NEWCASTLE
The Phanseys, c. 1645 (B.M. Add. MS. 32497)

LOVE LINE

My love is of a birth as rare
    As 'tis for object strange and high:
It was begotten by Despair
    Upon Impossibility.

Magnanimous Despair alone
    Could show me so divine a thing,
Where feeble Hope could ne'er have flown
    But vainly flapped its tinsel wing . . .

Unless the giddy heaven fall,
    And earth some new convulsion tear,
And, us to join, the world should all
    Be cramped into a planisphere.

As lines, so loves oblique may well
    Themselves in every angle greet:
But ours, so truly parallel,
    Though infinite can never meet.

Therefore the love which us doth bind,
    But Fate so enviously debars,
Is the conjunction of the mind,
    And opposition of the stars.

ANDREW MARVELL
Miscellaneous Poems, 1681 (written about 1650)

LOVE'S MATRIMONY

THERE is no happy life
But in a wife;
The comforts are so sweet
When they do meet:
'Tis plenty, peace, a calm
Like dropping balm:
Love's weather is so fair,
Perfumëd air,
Each word such pleasure brings
Like soft-touched strings;
Love's passion moves the heart
On either part.
Such harmony together,
So pleased in either,
No discords, concords still,
Sealed with one will.
By love, God man made one,
Yet not alone:
Like stamps of king and queen
It may be seen,
Two figures but one coin;
So they do join,
Only they not embrace,
We, face to face.

WILLIAM CAVENDISH, DUKE OF NEWCASTLE
The Phanseys, c. 1645 (B.M. Add. MS. 32497)

I LOVE
TO THINK OF THEE
I'll think of thee when
evening closes,
On a landscape bright
and fair,
I'll think of thee, when
hope reposes,
To claim a gift that
none can share.
When sleep on every eye-
lid hovers,
When every heart but
mine is free,
When darkness, earth and
ocean hovers,
Oh, then I love to think
of thee.

LIVERPOOL DELFT DISH *c.* 1760

CAPTIVE

I DID but look and love awhile,
   'Twas but for one half-hour;
Then to resist I had no will,
   And now I have no power.

THOMAS OTWAY
*The Works of Rochester and
Roscommon*, 1709

FACE TO FACE

WHEN our two souls stand up erect and strong,
Face to face, silent, drawing nigh and nigher,
Until the lengthening wings break into fire
At either curvëd point,—what bitter wrong
Can the earth do us, that we should not long
Be here contented? Think! In mounting higher,
The angels would press on us, and aspire
To drop some golden orb of perfect song
Into our deep, dear silence. Let us stay
Rather on earth, Belovëd—where the unfit
Contrarious moods of men recoil away
And isolate pure spirits, and permit
A place to stand and love in for a day,
With darkness and the death-hour rounding it.

ELIZABETH BARRETT BROWNING
Sonnets from the Portuguese, 1850

AND IS IT NIGHT?

AND is it night? Are they thine eyes that shine?
  Are we alone and here? and here alone?
May I come near? May I but touch thy shrine?
  Is jealousy asleep or is he gone?
O gods! no more silence my lips with thine,
Lips, kisses, joys, hap—blessings most divine.

Oh come, my dear, our griefs are turned to night,
  And night to joys: night blinds pale envy's eyes:
Silence and sleep prepare us our delight:
  Oh cease we then our woes, our griefs, our cries:
Oh vanish words! words do but passions move:
O dearest life, joy's sweet, O sweetest love!

ANONYMOUS, set to music by
Robert Jones in *A Musical Dream*, 1609

THE CHILD IN THE ROSE GARDEN

THERE is no rose of such vertu
As is the rose that bare Jesu.
    Alleluia.

For in this rose containëd was
Heaven and earth in little space:
    Res miranda.

By that rose we may well see
There be one God in persons three:
    Pares forma.

The angels sungen, the shepherds too:
Gloria in excelsis Deo:
    Gaudeamus.

Leave we all this worldly mirth,
And follow we this joyful birth:
    Transeamus.

ANONYMOUS
(fifteenth century)

NUNS: FRAGMENT OF FRESCO BY AMBROGIO LORENZETTI *c.* 1331

AFFECTION OF THE SPIRIT

A GREAT cry in the ears of God is this burning affection of the spirit, which saith: My God thou art my Love: thou art all mine and I am all thine. Enlarge me in love, that I may learn to taste with the inner mouth of the heart how sweet it is to love and to be melted and to swim in love.

Let me be possessed by Love, and lifted out of myself in the fervour of ecstasy.

I will sing the song of Love, I will follow thee, my Beloved, on high: my soul shall grow faint in thy praise, exulting in love.

THOMAS À KEMPIS
The Imitation of Christ, fifteenth century

LOVE be in my head, and in my understanding. Love be in mine eyes and in my looking. Love be in my mouth and in my speaking. Love be in my heart and in my thinking. Love be at mine end, and at my departing.

TRADITIONAL

OCTOBER TUNE

O LOVE, turn from the unchanging sea, and gaze
Down these grey slopes upon the year grown old,
A-dying mid the autumn-scented haze
That hangeth o'er the hollow in the wold,
Where the wind-bitten ancient elms infold
Grey church, long barn, orchard, and red-roofed stead,
Wrought in dead days for men a long while dead.

Come down, O love; may not our hands still meet,
Since still we live today, forgetting June,
Forgetting May, deeming October sweet—
—Oh hearken, hearken! through the afternoon,
The grey tower sings a strange old tinkling tune!
Sweet, sweet, and sad, the toiling year's last breath,
Too satiate of life to strive with death.

And we too—will it not be soft and kind,
That rest from life, from patience and from pain,
That rest from bliss we know not when we find,
That rest from love which ne'er the end can gain?—
—Hark, how the tune swells, that erewhile did wane!
Look up, love!—ah, cling close and never move!
How can I have enough of life and love?

WILLIAM MORRIS
The Earthly Paradise, 1870

THE FAITHFUL AND THE TRUE

LOVE lives beyond
The tomb, the earth, which fades like dew!
I love the fond,
The faithful, and the true.

Love lives in sleep,
The happiness of healthy dreams:
Eve's dews may weep,
But love delightful seems.

'Tis seen in flowers,
And in the morning's pearly dew;
In earth's green hours,
And in the heaven's eternal blue.

'Tis heard in Spring
When light and sunbeams, warm and kind,
On angel's wing
Bring love and music to the mind.

And where is voice,
So young, so beautiful, and sweet
As Nature's choice,
Where Spring and lovers meet?

Love lives beyond
The tomb, the earth, the flowers, and dew
I love the fond,
The faithful, young and true.

JOHN CLARE, *Life and Remains*, 1873

V: DREAMING

THERE is more pleasure in building castles in the air than on the ground.

EDWARD GIBBON, *Miscellaneous Works*, 1796

MAN is a *make-believe* animal—he is never so truly himself as when he is acting a part.

WILLIAM HAZLITT, *Notes of a Journey through France and Italy*, 1826

I SOMETIMES feel a little uneasy about that imagined self of mine—the Me of my daydreams—who leads a melodramatic life of his own, out of all relation with my real existence. So one day I shadowed him down the street. He loitered along for a while, and then stood at a shop-window and dressed himself out in a gaudy tie and yellow waistcoat. Then he bought a great sponge and two stuffed birds and took them to lodgings, where he led a shady existence. Next he moved to a big house in Mayfair, and gave grand dinner-parties, with splendid service and costly wines. His amorous adventures among the High-up Ones of this Earth I pass over. He soon sold his house and horses, gave up his motors, dismissed his retinue of servants, and went—saving two young ladies from being run over on the way—to live a life of heroic self-sacrifice among the poor.

I was beginning to feel encouraged about him, when in passing a fishmonger's, he pointed at a great salmon and said, 'I caught that fish'.

LOGAN PEARSALL SMITH, *Trivia*, 1918

WHEN my cousin and I took our porridge of a morning, we had a device to enliven the course of the meal. He ate his with sugar, and explained it to be a country continually buried under snow. I took mine with milk, and explained it to be a country suffering gradual inundation. You can imagine us exchanging bulletins; how here was an island still unsubmerged, here a valley not yet covered with snow; what inventions were made; how his population lived in cabins on perches and travelled on stilts, and how mine was always in boats; how the interest grew furious, as the last corner of safe ground was cut off on all sides and grew smaller every moment; and how, in fine, the food was of altogether secondary importance, and might even have been nauseous, so long as we seasoned it with these dreams. But perhaps the most exciting moments I ever had over a meal, were in the case of calves' foot jelly. It was hardly possible not to believe—and you may be sure, so far from trying, I did all I could to favour the illusion—that some part of it was hollow, and that sooner or later my spoon would lay open the secret tabernacle of the golden rock. There might some miniature Red Beard await his hour; there might one find the treasures of the Forty Thieves, and bewildered Cassim beating about the walls. And so I quarried on slowly, with bated breath, savouring the interest. Believe me, I had little palate left for the jelly; and though I preferred the taste when I took cream with it, I used often to go without, because the cream dimmed the transparent fractures.

ROBERT LOUIS STEVENSON
Virginibus Puerisque, 1881

TRANSFORMATION SCENES

ONE morning when I was in the wood something happened which was nothing less than a transformation of myself and the world, although I 'believed' nothing new. I was looking at a great, spreading, bursting oak. The first tinge from the greenish-yellow buds was just visible. It seemed to be no longer a tree away from me and apart from me. The enclosing barriers of consciousness were removed and the text came into my mind, 'Thou in me and I in Thee'. The distinction of self and not-self was an illusion. I could feel the rising sap; in me also sprang the fountain of life uprushing from its roots, and the joy of its outbreak at the extremity of each twig right up to the summit was my own: that which kept me apart was nothing.

MARK RUTHERFORD
More Pages from a Journal, 1910

WHEN I was but thirteen or so
    I went into a golden land
Chimborazo, Cotopaxi
    Took me by the hand.

My father died, my brother too,
    They passed like fleeting dreams,
I stood where Popocatapetl
    In the sunlight gleams.

I dimly heard the master's voice
    And boys far-off at play,
Chimborazo, Cotopaxi
    Had stolen me away.

186

I walked in a great golden dream
  To and fro from school—
Shining Popocatapetl
  The dusty streets did rule.

I walked home with a gold dark boy
  And never a word I'd say,
Chimborazo, Cotopaxi
  Had taken my speech away:

I gazed entranced upon his face
  Fairer than any flower—
O shining Popocatapetl
  It was thy magic hour:

The houses, people, traffic seemed
  Thin fading dreams by day,
Chimborazo, Cotopaxi
  They had stolen my soul away!

w. j. turner, *The Hunter*, 1916

THE MOOD OF DREAM

ALL day long the door of the sub-conscious remains just ajar; we slip through to the other side, and return again, as easily and secretly as a cat. A dreamlike mood will haunt the mind as moonlight through a window haunts a room, or the sense of disquietude and foreboding that foretells a storm. Obsessive memories vividly imagined, welcome or unwelcome, will insinuate themselves into our active and open thoughts, and so at length decoy our attention to them. As may the distant singing of a bird which the ear, at first refusing to heed, at length cannot evade; as does the shadow-barred light on the wall in Rembrandt's picture—patiently waiting until St. Jerome peers up from his great open book to welcome its company. Any glimpse of unexpected beauty, that of a lovely face, or of a serene landscape, its hollows receding beyond low hills, or of a tranquil daybreak and an eastern sky with its dove-grey low-lying lattice of clouds, the pale blue as of an infinite peace between them— all such things, even an abstracted moment with a pebble, a tea-cup, or a blade of grass, may still the waking mind, and so are reminiscent of the more tranquil and moving of our dreams.

WALTER DE LA MARE, *Behold, this Dreamer!* 1939

THE PHILOSOPHER: PAINTING BY REMBRANDT VAN RIJN *c.* 1630

GREENWICH (DETAIL): PAINTING BY J. J. J. TISSOT

DAY-DREAMING

THIS placid pastime—snare of the idle, scorn of the matter-of-fact—deserves a slender anthology all to itself. It has indeed been recent scrutinized, dissected, and tabulated in more than one treatise slender neither in bulk nor augmentation. Compared with dream, it is what nectar is to honey, tint to colour. It resembles, in its gentle rilling, the circulation of the blood; and *may* be the usual occupation, apart from the needs and dangers of their workaday existence, of bird and beast and fish. A passive looking-glass-life of action reflections—the cow in the meadow, the sheep in the corn. A Painted Lady perched on a flower; a thrush in tranced meditation on her nest; a drowsy cat on her footstool by the fire, are, at least, pictures and emblems of reverie; and a great deal more of our workaday life is spent in this heedless industry than we are likely to realize, or might care to confess. The enjoyment of every tale, of every poem we read, indeed, is largely in the nature of a day-dream, even though it is being built up in an astonishing fashion out of a purely verbal fabric. Every hope, every expectation, every desire and resolve concerning that radiant or dismal region of the life of the mind which we call the Future, and which, in general, might be more precisely designated as the Never-Never-Land, also resembles a day-dream—suspended, like dew-drops, on filaments of fact and truth and fancy, spun out of the silk of memory, and even more flimsy, if no less attractive in design, than a spider's web. 'That it was May, thus dremëd', whispers romance, and Cupid creeps a little closer with his dart.

WALTER DE LA MARE, *Behold, this Dreamer!* 1939

THE RULE OF IMAGINATION

MEN are ruled by imagination: imagination makes them into men, capable of madness and of immense labours. We work dreaming. Consider what dreams must have dominated the builders of the Pyramids—dreams geometrical, dreams funereal, dreams of resurrection, dreams of outdoing the pyramid of some other Pharaoh! What dreams occupy that fat man in the street, toddling by under his shabby hat and bedraggled rain-coat? Perhaps he is in love; perhaps he is a Catholic, and imagines that early this morning he has partaken of the body and blood of Christ; perhaps he is a revolutionist, with the millenium in his heart and a bomb in his pocket. The spirit bloweth where it listeth; the wind of inspiration carries our dreams before it and constantly refashions them like clouds. Nothing could be madder, more irresponsible, more dangerous than this guidance of men by dreams. What saves us is the fact that our imaginations, groundless and chimerical as they may seem, are secretly suggested and controlled by shrewd old instincts of our animal nature, and by continual contact with things. The shock of sense, breaking in upon us with a fresh irresistible image, checks wayward imagination and sends it rebounding in a new direction, perhaps more relevant to what is happening in the world outside.

When I speak of being governed by imagination, of course I am indulging in a figure of speech, in an ellipsis; in reality we are governed by that perpetual latent process within us by which imagination itself is created. Actual imaginings—the cloud-like thoughts drifting by—are not masters over themselves nor over anything else. They are like the sound of chimes in the night; they know nothing of whence they came, how they will fall out, or how long they will ring. There is a mechanism in the church tower; there was a theme in the composer's head; there is a beadle who has been winding the thing up. The sound wafted to us, muffled by distance and a thousand obstacles, is but the last lost emanation of this magical bell-ringing. Yet in our dream it is all in all; it is what first entertains and absorbs the mind. Imagination, when it chimes within us, apparently of itself, is no less elaborately grounded; it is a last symptom, a rolling echo, by which we detect and name the obscure operaton that occasions it; and not this echo in its aesthetic impotence, but the whole operation whose last witness it is, receives in science the name of imagination, and may be truly said to rule the human world . . .

Whilst dreams entertain us, the balance of our character is shifting beneath: we are growing while we sleep. The young think in one way, the drunken in another, and the dead not at all; and I imagine—for I have imagination myself—that they do not die because they stop thinking, but they stop thinking because they die. How much veering and luffing before they make that port! The brain of man, William James used to say, has a hair-trigger organization. His life is terribly experimental. He is perilously dependent on the oscillations of a living needle, imagination, that never points to the true north . . .

Imagination changes the scale of everything, and makes a thousand patterns of the woof of nature, without disturbing a single thread. Or rather—since it is nature itself that imagines—it turns to music what was only strain; as if the universal vibration, suddenly ashamed of having been so long silent and useless, had burst into tears and laughter at its own folly, and in so doing had become wise.

GEORGE SANTAYANA, *Soliloquies in England*, 1922

THE FLICKERING SHADE

FLUTTER of something in the past, that made
A light of white across the flickering shade;
    That passed us near, but will come back no more.

Shudder of something in the days that are;
Possible music in sweet notes that jar:
    And not unlike some notes we heard before.

Visible glimpses of old robes again:
Audible echoes of old sounds, with pain
    And distance touched, but playing o'er and o'er.

As if love might have been, and has not been:
As if love yet, though faint, in hope were seen:
    A far, faint flicker, down a lonely shore.

O follow, follow, and find it! o'er the slope
Of matted sands, before the tide come up!
    Ere night close soon, and it be seen no more!

THOMAS ASHE, *Dryope*, 1861

DREAM BIRD

WHEN a dream is born in you
   With a sudden clamorous pain,
When you know the dream is true
   And lovely, with no flaw nor stain,
O then, be careful, or with sudden clutch
You'll hurt the delicate thing you prize so much.

Dreams are like a bird that mocks,
   Flirting the feathers of his tail.
When you seize at the salt-box
   Over the hedge you'll see him sail.
Old birds are neither caught with salt nor chaff:
They watch you from the apple bough and laugh.

Poet, never chase the dream.
   Laugh yourself and turn away.
Mask your hunger, let it seem
   Small matter is he come or stay;
But when he nestles in your hand at last,
Close up your fingers tight and hold him fast.

ROBERT GRAVES, 'A Pinch of Salt'
Fairies and Fusiliers, 1917

THE FLAME IN THE PETALS

. . . As he walked one evening, a garden gate, usually closed, stood open; and lo! within, a great red hawthorn, in full flower, embossing heavily the bleached and twisted trunk and branches, so aged that there were but few green leaves thereon—a plumage of tender, crimson fire out of the heart of the dry wood. The perfume of the tree had now and again reached him, in the currents of the wind, over the wall, and he had wondered what might be behind it, and was now allowed to fill his arms with the flowers—flowers enough for all the old blue-china pots along the chimney-piece, making fête in the children's room. Was it some periodic moment in the expansion of soul within him, or mere trick of heat in the heavily-laden summer air? But the beauty of the thing struck home to him feverishly, and in dreams, all night, he loitered along a magic roadway of crimson flowers, which seemed to open ruddily in thick, fresh masses about his feet, and fill softly all the little hollows in the banks on either side. Always, afterwards, summer by summer, as the flowers came on, the blossom of the red hawthorn still seemed to him absolutely the reddest of all things; and the goodly crimson, still alive in the works of old Venetian masters, or old Flemish tapestries, called out always from afar the recollection of the flame in those perishing little petals, as it pulsed gradually out of them, kept long in the drawers of an old cabinet.

WALTER PATER, *The Child in the House*, 1894

198

KUBLA KHAN

In the summer of the year 1797, the Author, then in ill health, had retired to a lonely farm-house between Portlock and Linton, on the Exmoor confines of Somerset and Devonshire. In consequence of a slight indisposition an anodyne had been prescribed, from the effects of which he fell asleep in his chair at the moment that he was reading the following sentence, or words of the same substance, in Purchas's Pilgrimage: 'Here the Khan Kubla commanded a palace to be built, and a stately garden thereunto. And thus ten miles of fertile ground were enclosed with a wall.' The author continued for about three hours in a profound sleep, at least of the external senses, during which time he has the most vivid confidence that he could not have composed less than from two to three hundred lines; if that indeed can be called composition in which all the images rose up before him as things, with a parallel production of the correspondent expressions, without any sensation or consciousness of effort. On awaking he appeared to himself to have a distinct recollection of the whole, and taking his pen, ink, and paper, instantly and eagerly wrote down the lines that are here preserved. At this moment he was unfortunately called out by a person on business from Portlock, and detained by him above an hour, and on his return to his room, found, to his no small surprise and mortification, that though he still retained some vague and dim recollection of the general purport of the vision, yet, with the exception of some eight or ten scattered lines and images, all the rest had passed away like the images on the surface of a stream into which a stone has been cast, but, alas! without the after-restoration of the latter!

SAMUEL TAYLOR COLERIDGE
Biographia Literaria, 1817

VI : MAKING

Louis Dubedat: I believe in Michael Angelo, Velasquez, and Rembrandt; in the might of design, the mystery of colour, the redemption of all things by Beauty everlasting, and the message of Art that has made these hands blessed. Amen.

BERNARD SHAW, *The Doctor's Dilemma*, 1906

If a man love the labour of any trade, apart from any question of success or fame, the gods have called him.

ROBERT LOUIS STEVENSON

The sound of tools to a clever workman who loves his work is like the tentative sounds of the orchestra to the violinist who has to bear his part in the overture; the strong fibres begin their accustomed thrill, and what was a moment before joy, vexation or ambition, begins its change into energy. All passion becomes strength when it has an outlet from the narrow limits of our personal lot in the labour of our right arm, the cunning of our right hand, or the still, creative activity of our thought.

GEORGE ELIOT, *Adam Bede*, 1859

A tool is but the extension of a man's hand, and a machine is but a complex tool, and he that invents a machine augments the power of a man.

HENRY WARD BEECHER

CECKING THE MAIN SHAFT OF THE GEAR-BOX OF A ROLLS-ROYCE ENGINE ON A PROFILE MACHINE
OTOGRAPH BY ZOLTAN GLASS

THE LACE-MAKER: PAINTING BY CASPAR NETSCHER 1664

THE ARTIST'S INSIGHT

WE carve and paint, or we behold what is carved and painted, as students of the mystery of Form. The virtue of art lies in detachment, in sequestering one object from the embarrassing variety. Until one thing comes out from the connection of things, there can be enjoyment, contemplation, but no thought. Our happiness and unhappiness are unproductive. The infant lies in a pleasing trance, but his individual character and his practical power depend on his daily progress in the separation of things, and dealing with one at a time. Love and all the passions concentrate all existence around a single form. It is the habit of certain minds to give an all-excluding fullness to the object, the thought, the word, they alight upon, and to make that for the time the deputy of the world. These are the artists, the orators, the leaders of society. The power to detach, and to magnify by detaching, is the essence of rhetoric in the hands of the orator and the poet. This rhetoric, or power to fix the momentary eminency of an object,—so remarkable in Burke, in Byron, in Carlyle,—the painter and sculptor exhibit in colour and in stone. The power depends on the depth of the artist's insight of that object he contemplates. For every object has its roots in central nature, and may of course be so exhibited to us as to represent the world.

RALPH WALDO EMERSON
Essays, 1841

AN artist is a dreamer consenting to dream of the actual world.

GEORGE SANTAYANA

BEGINNINGS

I WAS for some time kept at reading, writing, and figures—how long, I know not, but I know that as soon as my question was done upon my slate, I spent as much time as I could in filling with my pencil all the unoccupied spaces, with representations of such objects as struck my fancy; and these were rubbed out, for fear of a beating, before my question was given in. As soon as I reached Fractions, Decimals, &c., I was put to learn Latin . . . I rather flagged in this department of my education, and the margins of my books, and every space of spare and blank paper, became filled with various kinds of devices or scenes I had met with; and these were accompanied with wretched rhymes explanatory of them. As soon as I filled all the blank spaces in my books, I had recourse, at all spare times, to the gravestones and the floor of the church porch, with a bit of chalk, to give vent to this propensity of mind of figuring whatever I had seen. At that time I had never heard of the word 'drawing'; nor did I know of any other paintings besides the King's arms in the church, and the signs in Ovingham of the Black Bull, the White Horse, the Salmon, and the Hounds and Hare. I always thought I could make a far better hunting scene than the latter: the others were beyond my hand. I remember once of my master overlooking me while I was very busy with my chalk in the porch, and of his putting me very greatly to the blush by ridiculing me and calling me a conjurer. My father, also, found a deal of fault for 'mispending my time in such idle pursuits'; but my propensity for drawing was so rooted that nothing could deter me from persevering in it; and many of my evenings at home were spent in filling the flags of the floor and the hearth-stone with my chalky designs.

THOMAS BEWICK
A Memoir . . . written by Himself, 1862

ACHIEVEMENTS

It was on the day, or rather night, of the 27th of June, 1787, between the hours of eleven and twelve, that I wrote the last lines of the last page, in a summer house in my garden. After laying down my pen I took several turns in a *berceau*, or covered walk of acacias, which commands a prospect of the country, the lake and mountains. The air was temperate, the sky was serene, the silver orb of the moon was reflected from the waters, and all nature was silent. I will not dissemble the first emotions of joy on recovery of my freedom, and perhaps, the establishment of my fame. But my pride was soon humbled, and a sober melancholy was spread over my mind, by the idea that I had taken an everlasting leave of an old and agreeable companion, and that, whatsoever might be the future date of my History, the life of the historian must be short and precarious.

EDWARD GIBBON, *Memoirs*, 1796

The discovery of the two optically active tartaric acids was a momentous one, effecting a revolution in the views of chemists regarding molecular structure; and we can well understand the feeling of happiness and the nervous excitement by which Pasteur was overcome on making his discovery. Rushing from his laboratory and meeting a curator he embraced him, exclaiming, 'I have just made a great discovery! I have separated the sodium ammonium parotartrate into two salts of opposite action on the plane of polarization of light. The dextro-salt is in all respects identical with the dextro-tartrate. I am so happy and overcome by such nervous excitement that I am unable to place my eye again to the polarization apparatus.'

ALEXANDER FINDLAY, *Chemistry in the Service of Man*, 1916

I CARRY my ideas about me for a long time, often a very long time, before I commit them to writing. My memory is so good that I never forget a theme that has once come to me, even if it is a matter of years. I alter much, reject, try again until I am satisfied. Then, in my head, the thing develops in all directions, and, since I know precisely what I want, the original idea never eludes me. It rises before me, grows, I hear it, see it in all its size and extension, standing before me like a cast, and it only remains for me to write it down, which is soon done when I can find the time, for sometimes I take up other work, though I never confuse that with the other. You will ask where I find my ideas: I hardly know. They come uninvited, directly or indirectly. I can almost grasp them with my hands in the open air, in the woods, while walking, in the stillness of the night, early in the morning, called up by moods which the poet translates into words, I into musical tones. They ring and roar and swirl about me until I write them down in notes.

> LUDWIG VON BEETHOVEN
> Recorded in Alexander Wheelock Thayer's *Life*, 1866

HE is the only person I ever knew who answered to the idea of a man of genius . . . His voice rolled on the ear like the pealing organ, and its sound alone was the music of thought. His mind was clothed with wings; and, raised on them, he lifted philosophy to heaven. In his descriptions, you then saw the progress of human happiness and liberty in bright and never-ending succession, like the steps of Jacob's ladder, with airy shapes ascending and descending, and with the voice of God at the top of the ladder . . .

> WILLIAM HAZLITT, on Coleridge
> *Lectures on the English Poets*, 1818

GATHERED RAYS

WE will entangle buds and flowers and beams
Which twinkle on the fountain's brim, and make
Strange combinations out of common things,
Like human babes in their brief innocence;
And we will search, with looks and words of love,
For hidden thoughts, each lovelier than the last,
Our unexhausted spirits; and like lutes,
Touched by the skill of the enamoured wind,
Weave harmonies divine, yet ever new,
From difference sweet where discord cannot be;
And hither come, sped on the charmèd winds,
Which meet from all the points of heaven, as bees
From every flower aereal Enna feeds,
At their known island-homes in Himera,
The echoes of the human world, which tell
Of the low voice of love, almost unheard,
And dove-eyed pity's murmured pain, and music,
Itself the echo of the heart, and all
That tempers or improves man's life, now free;
And lovely apparitions,—dim at first,
Then radiant, as the mind, arising bright
From the embrace of beauty (whence the forms
Of which these are the phantoms) casts on them
The gathered rays which are reality—
Shall visit us, the progeny immortal
Of Painting, Sculpture, and rapt Poesy,
And arts, though unimagined, yet to be.

PERCY BYSSHE SHELLEY
Prometheus Unbound, 1820

THE POET

FOR me there is no dismay
Though ills enough impend.
I have learned to count each day
Minute by breathing minute—
Birds that lightly begin it,
Shadows muting its end—
As lovers count for luck
Their own heart-beats and believe
In the forest of time they pluck
Eternity's single leaf.

Tonight the moon's at the full.
Full moon's the time for murder.
But I look to the clouds that hide her—
The bay below me is dull,
An unreflecting glass—
And chafe for the clouds to pass,
And wish she suddenly might
Blaze down at me so I shiver
Into a twelve-branched river
Of visionary light.

For now imagination,
My royal, impulsive swan,
With raking flight—I can see her—
Comes down as it were upon
A lake in whirled snow-floss
And flurry of spray like a skier
Checking.   Again I feel
The wounded waters heal.

Never before did she cross
My heart with such exaltation.

Oh, on this striding edge,
This hare-bell height of calm
Where intuitions swarm
Like nesting gulls and knowledge
Is free as the winds that blow,
A little while sustain me,
Love, till my answer is heard!
Oblivion roars below,
Death's cordon narrows: but vainly,
If I've slipped the carrier word.

Dying, any man may
Feel wisdom harmonious, fateful
At the tip of his dry tongue.
All I have felt or sung
Seems now but the moon's fitful
Sleep on a clouded bay,
Swan's maiden flight, or the climb
To a tremulous, hare-bell crest.
Love, tear the song from my breast!
Short, short is the time.

CECIL DAY LEWIS
Poems in Wartime, 1940

THE FARMER

But turn, my Muse, nor let th'alluring form
Of beauty lead too far thy devious steps.
See where the farmer, with a master's eye,
Surveys his little kingdom, and exults
In sov'reign independence. At a word,
His feathery subjects in obedience flock
Around his feeding hand, who in return
Yield a delicious tribute to his board,
And o'er his couch their downy plumage spread.
The peacock here expands his eyeful plumes,
A glittering pageant, to the mid-day sun:
In the stiff awkwardness of foolish pride,
The swelling turkey apes his stately step,
And calls the bristling feathers round his head.
There the loud herald of the morning struts
Before his cackling dames, the passive slaves
Of his promiscuous pleasure. O'er the pond,
See the grey gander, with his female train,
Bending their lofty necks; and gabbling ducks,
Rejoicing on the surface clap their wings;
Whilst wheeling round, in airy wanton flights,
The glossy pigeons chase their sportive loves,
Or in soft cooings tell their amorous tale.
Here stacks of hay, there pyramids of corn,
Promise the future market large supplies:
While with an eye of triumph he surveys
His piles of wood, and laughs at winter's frown . . .

ROBERT DODSLEY, *Public Virtue*, 1753

HARVESTING IN BRIT
PAINTING BY PAUL GAUGUIN,

SILVER COFFEE POT BY JOHN ELSTON, EXETER 1716

THE CRAFTSMAN

. . . AND in the heat of the furnace will he wrestle with his work: the noise of the hammer will be in his ear, and his eyes upon the pattern of the vessel; he will set his heart upon perfecting his works . . .

Ecclesiasticus

Things men have made with wakened hands, and put soft life into are awake through years with transferred touch, and go on glowing for long years.
And for this reason, some old things are lovely,
warm still with the life of forgotten men who made them.

D. H. LAWRENCE, *Pansies*, 1929

THE first blow of the domed hammer into the virgin whiteness of the metal; the rhythmic beating of steel hammer to steel anvil—making the metal obey his will and bringing the inert, flat, circular piece of metal up to a faultless body of a drinking cup, a chalice, or a large fruit or flower bowl; the choice of strengthening wires made on a draw bench as it was three hundred years ago; the extreme care and patience necessary to fit the base to the body; the feeling of fire responding to his will when fusing the two parts together; its cleanliness of working, for there is no dross when handling silver; the exhilaration of decorating by engraving or chasing; and finally the feel of the finished piece—all these are the simple joys of the craftsman.

LESLIE DURBIN
in *Fifteen Craftsmen on their Crafts*, 1948

THE GARDENER

THE most exquisite delights of sense are pursued in the contrivance and planning of gardens, which, with fruits, flowers, shades, fountains, and the music of birds that frequent such happy places, seem to furnish all the pleasures of the several senses, and with the greatest, or at least the most natural perfections.

SIR WILLIAM TEMPLE, *Miscellanea*, 1690

Is it not a pleasant sight to behold a multitude of trees round about, in decent form and order, bespangled and gorgeously apparelled with green leaves, blooms and goodly fruits as with a rich robe of embroidered work, or as hanging with some precious and costly jewels or pearls, the boughs laden and burdened, bowing down to you, and freely offering their ripe fruits as a large satisfaction of all your labours?

RALPH AUSTEN, *A Treatise of Fruit-Trees*, 1653

ALL the wars of the world, all the Caesars, have not the staying power of a lily in a cottage border . . . The immortality of marbles and of miseries is a vain, small thing compared to the immortality of a flower that blooms and is dead by dusk.

REGINALD FARRER, *The Rainbow Bridge*, 1921

THAT border was a dream in June. It is going to be lovely again in October.

RUTH DRAPER

THE GARDENER

I took money and bought flowering trees
And planted them out on the bank to the east of the Keep.
I simply bought whatever had most blooms,
Not caring whether peach, apricot, or plum.
A hundred fruits, all mixed up together;
A thousand branches, flowering in due rotation.
Each has its season coming early or late;
But to all alike the fertile soil is kind.
The red flowers hang like a heavy mist;
The white flowers gleam like a fall of snow.
The wandering bees cannot bear to leave them;
The sweet birds also come there to roost.
In front there flows an ever-running stream;
Beneath there is built a little flat terrace.
Sometimes I sweep the flagstones of the terrace;
Sometimes, in the wind, I raise my cup and drink.
The flower-branches screen my head from the sun;
The flower-buds fall down into my lap.
Alone drinking, alone singing my songs,
I do not notice that the moon is level with the steps.
The people of Pa do not care for flowers;
All the spring no one has come to look.
But their Governor-General, alone with his cup of wine,
Sits till evening, and will not move from the place!

Written when Governor of Chung-Chou by
PO-CHÜ-I, translated by ARTHUR WALEY
170 Chinese Poems, 1920

THE BUILDERS

WE have graven the mountain of God with hands,
As our hands were graven of God, they say,
Where the seraphs burn in the sun like brands
And the devils carry the rains away:
Making a thrift of the throats of hell,
Our gargoyles gather the roaring rain,
Whose yawn is more than a frozen yell
And their very vomiting not in vain . . .

We have graven the forest of heaven with hands,
Being great with a mirth too gross for pride,
In the stone that battered him Stephen stands
And Peter himself is petrified:
Such hands as have grubbed in the glebe for bread
Have bidden the blank rock blossom and thrive,
Such hands as have stricken a live man dead
Have struck, and stricken the dead alive . . .

Fold your hands before heaven in praying,
Lift up your hands into heaven and cry;
But look where our dizziest spires are saying
What the hands of a man did up in the sky:
Drenched before you have heard the thunder,
White before you have felt the snow;
For the giants lift up their heads to wonder
How high the hands of a man could go.

G. K. CHESTERTON
The Ballad of St Barbara and Other Verses, 1922

216

ENTRANCE TO A LANE: PAINTING BY GRAHAM SUTHERLAND 1939

VII: UNDERSTANDING

To walk abroad is, not with eyes,
But thoughts, the fields to see and prize;
   Else may the silent feet,
     Like logs of wood,
Move up and down, and see no good,
   Nor joy nor glory meet.

Ev'n carts and wheels their place do change,
But cannot see, though very strange
   The glory that is by:
     Dead puppets may
Move in the bright and glorious day,
   Yet not behold the sky.

And are not men than they more blind,
Who having eyes yet never find
   The bliss in which they move?
     Like statues dead
They up and down are carriëd,
   Yet neither see nor love.

To walk is by a thought to go,
To move in spirit to and fro,
   To mind the good we see,
     To taste the sweet,
Observing all the things we meet
   How choice and rich they be . . .

THOMAS TRAHERNE, *Poems of Felicity*, 1903 (written *c.* 1670)

PASSION

FULL of desire I lay, the sky wounding me,
Each cloud a ship without me sailing, each tree
Possessing what my soul lacked, tranquillity.

Waiting for the longed-for voice to speak
Through the mute telephone, my body grew weak
With the well-known and mortal death, heartbreak.

The language I knew best, my human speech
Forsook my fingers, and out of reach
Were Homer's ghosts, the savage conches of the beach.

Then the sky spoke to me in language clear,
Familiar as the heart, than love more near.
The sky said to my soul, 'You have what you desire!

'Know now that you are born along with these
Clouds, winds, and stars, and ever-moving seas
And forest dwellers. This your nature is.

Lift up your heart again without fear,
Sleep in the tomb, or breathe the living air,
This world you with the flower and with the tiger share.'

Then I saw every visible substance turn
Into immortal, every cell new born
Burned with the holy fire of passion.

This world I saw as on her judgment day
When the war ends, and the sky rolls away,
And all is light, love and eternity.

KATHLEEN RAINE, Stone and Flower, 1943

A COMMON SPIRIT

WHEN the soul attends through her proper faculty, she is instantly carried away into the other world of purity, eternity, immortality and of unchanging things; and there finding her own element she merges herself in it (that is, so long as she is true to herself and keeps herself whole); and she strays no longer, but thus always in regard to it she remains steadfast, for that also in which she has merged herself is steadfast. And the name of this condition of the Soul is Understanding.

PLATO, *Phaedo*

I AM sure there is a common spirit that plays within us, yet makes no part of us; and that is, the Spirit of God, the fire and scintillation of that noble and mighty Essence, which is the life and radical heat of Spirits, and those essences that know not the vertue of the Sun; a fire quite contrary to the fire of Hell. This is that gentle heat that brooded on the waters, and in six days hatched the World; this is that irradiation that dispels the mists of Hell, the clouds of horror, fear, sorrow, despair, and preserves the region of the mind in serenity. Whosoever feels not the warm gale and gentle ventilation of this Spirit, though I feel his pulse, I dare not say he lives: for truly, without this, there is no heat under the Tropick; nor any light, though I dwelt in the body of the Sun.

SIR THOMAS BROWNE, *Religio Medici*, 1642

CONGREGATION

As with great fervour he was going on the way, he lifted up his eyes and beheld some trees hard by the road, whereon sat a great company of birds wellnigh without number; whereat Saint Francis marvelled, and said to his companions: 'Ye shall wait for me here upon the way and I will go to preach unto my little sisters, the birds'. And he went unto the field and began to preach unto the birds that were on the ground; and immediately those that were on the trees flew down to him, and they all of them remained still and quiet together, until Saint Francis made an end of preaching . . . The sermon preached unto them was after this fashion: 'My little sisters, the birds, much bounden are ye unto God, your Creator, and always in every place ought ye to praise Him, for that He hath given you liberty to fly about everywhere, and hath also given you double and triple raiment; moreover He preserved your seed in the ark of Noah, that your race might not perish out of the world; still more are ye beholden to Him for the element of the air which He hath appointed for you; beyond all this, ye sow not, neither do you reap; and God feedeth you, and giveth you the streams and fountains for your drink; the mountains and the valleys for your refuge and the high trees whereon to make your nests; and because ye know not how to spin or sew, God clotheth you, you and your children; wherefore your Creator loveth you much, seeing that He hath bestowed on you so many benefits; and therefore, my little sisters, beware of the sin of ingratitude, and study always to give praises unto God'. Whenas Saint Francis spake these words to them, those birds began all of them to open their beaks, and stretch their necks, and spread their wings, and reverently bend their heads down to the ground, and by their acts and by their songs to show that the holy Father gave them joy exceeding great.

SAINT FRANCIS OF ASSISI, *Fioretti*, translated by T. W. Arnold

Cy commence le douzieme
livre des proprietes des chose
oual toute premierement
des oyseaulx en general · et
apres en particulier.

Puis que nous a
nous ou premier
volume dit et
ue de lair · et de
impressions qui y sont en
stendues · maintenant ap
partient et nous reste de

dire auant chose de ce qui
affiert a son mouuement.
A celle fin que la maiesste
de et puissance du createur
soit en eulx loe et maigni
fiee comme es autres crea
tures · A sauoir ement
de lair doncques appartient
les oyseaulx et toute chose
qui volent · si comme dist
de le venerable · Et pour
ce a layde de dieu nous en
dirons vnch peu de chose

BARTHOLOMAEUS ANGLICUS AND THE BIRDS: FLEMISH MANUSCRIPT, c. 1482

PEACE

I SOUGHT for Peace, but could not find;
  I sought it in the city,
But they were of another mind,
  The more's the pity!

I sought for Peace of country swain,
  But yet I could not find;
So I, returning home again,
  Left Peace behind.

Sweet Peace, where dost thou dwell? said I.
  Methought a voice was given;
Peace dwelt not here, long since did fly
  To God in Heaven.

Thought I, this echo is but vain,
  To folly 'tis of kin;
Anon I heard it tell me plain,
  'Twas killed by sin.

Then I believed the former voice,
  And rested well content,
Laid down and slept, rose, did rejoice,
  And then to heaven went.
There I enquired for Peace, and found it true,
An heavenly plant it was, and sweetly grew.

SAMUEL SPEED, *Prison Piety*, 1677

RCH
SAN SPIRITO
IGENTO, SICILY

LAST SONG

I HAVE loved flowers that fade,
Within whose magic tents
Rich hues have marriage made
With sweet unmemoried scents:
A honeymoon delight—
A joy of love at sight,
That ages in an hour:
My song be like a flower!

I have loved airs, that die
Before their charm is writ
Along a liquid sky
Trembling to welcome it.
Notes, that with pulse of fire
Proclaim the spirit's desire,
Then die, and are nowhere:
My song be like an air!

Die, song, die like a breath,
And wither as a bloom:
Fear not a flowery death,
Dread not an airy tomb!
Fly with delight, fly hence!
'Twas thine love's tender sense
To feast; now on thy bier
Beauty shall shed a tear.

ROBERT BRIDGES, *Shorter Poems*, 1890

226

GOD'S GRANDEUR

THE world is charged with the grandeur of God,
  It will flame out, like shining from shook foil;
  It gathers to a greatness, like the ooze of oil
Crushed. Why do men then now not reck his rod?
Generations have trod, have trod, have trod;
  And all is seared with trade; bleared, smeared with toil;
  And wears man's smudge and shares man's smell: the soil
Is bare now, nor can foot feel, being shod.

And for all this, nature is never spent;
  There lives the dearest freshness deep down things;
And though the last lights off the black West went
  Oh, morning, at the brown brink eastward, springs—
Because the Holy Ghost over the bent
  World broods with warm breast and with ah! bright wings.

GERARD MANLEY HOPKINS
Poems, 1930 (written 1877)

GOD, in the whizzing of a pleasant wind,
Shall march upon the tops of mulberry trees.

GEORGE PEELE, *David and Bethsabe,* 1599

VIII: FALLING ASLEEP

SLEEPY, my dear? Yes, yes, I see
Morpheus is fall'n in love with thee;
Morpheus, my worst of rivals, tries
To draw the curtains of thine eyes,
And fans them with his wing asleep,
Makes drowsy love play at bo-peep;
How prettily his feathers blow
Those fleshy shuttings to and fro!
Oh how he makes me tantalize
With those fair apples of thine eyes,
Equivocates and cheats me still,
Opening and shutting at his will;
Now both, now one, the doting god
Plays with thine eyes at even-and-odd:
My stammering tongue doubts which it might
Bid thee—Good morrow, or Good night;
So thy eyes twinkle, brighter far
Than the bright, trembling evening star;
So a wax taper, burnt within
The socket, plays at out and in.

NATHANIEL HOOKES, *Amanda*, 1653

ONE by one the flowers close,
Lily and dewy rose
Shutting their tender petals from the moon:
The grasshoppers are still; but not so soon
   Are still the noisy crows.

The dormouse squats and eats
Choice little dainty bits
Beneath the spreading roots of a broad lime;
Nibbling his fill he stops from time to time
   And listens where he sits.

From far the lowings come
Of cattle driven home:
From farther still the wind brings fitfully
The vast continual murmur of the sea,
   Now loud, now almost dumb . . .

Hark! that's the nightingale,
Telling the selfsame tale
Her song told when this ancient earth was young;
So echoes answered when her song was sung
   In the first wooded vale.

We call it love and pain
The passion of her strain;
And yet we little understand or know:
Why should it not be rather joy that so
   Throbs in each throbbing vein?

CHRISTINA ROSSETTI, from 'Twilight Calm'
Goblin Market and other Poems, 1862

SETTING BY PETER WARLOCK

thence There may steal an in-fluence All — my powers of care be-
reav—ing.

I I

Though but a shadow, but a sliding,
Let me know some little joy!
We, that suffer long annoy,
Are contented with a thought
Through an idle fancy wrought:
O let my joys have some abiding!

WORDS BY FRANCIS BEAUMONT, *The Woman-Hater*, 1607

BED

FOR do but consider what an excellent thing sleep is. It is so inestimable a jewel that if a Tyrant would give his crown for an hour's slumber it cannot be bought. Of so beautiful a shape is it that though a man lie with an Empress his heart cannot be at quiet till he leaves her embracements to be at rest with the other. Yea, so greatly indebted are we to this kinsman of death that we owe the better tributary, half of our life, to him: and there is good cause why we should do so, for sleep is that golden chain that ties health and our bodies together. Who complains of want, of wounds, of cares, of great men's oppressions, of captivity, whilst he sleepeth? Beggars in their beds take as much pleasure as kings. Can we therefore surfeit on this delicate ambrosia?

THOMAS DEKKER, *The Gul's Horn-booke*, 1609

My bed, the rest of all my cares,
  The end of toiling pain,
Which bringest ease and solace sweet,
  While darkness doth remain;
My bed, yield to me slumber sweet,
  And trifling dreams repel;
Cause carking care from sobbing breast
  To part, where it doth dwell;
All mockeries of this wretched world
  Put clean from out my mind:
Do these, my bed, and then by thee
  Much comfort shall I find.

TIMOTHY KENDALL
Flowers of Epigrams, 1577

232

OAK BED AT OCKWELLS MANOR, BERKSHIRE, *c.* 1615

THE LAKE FROM PETWORTH HOUSE, SUNSET (DETAIL): PAINTING BY J. M. W. TURNER, R.A., *c.* 1829

SUNSET

THE golden eve is all astir,
The tides of sunset flood on us
—Incredible, miraculous—
We look with adoration on
Beauty coming, beauty gone,
That waits not any looking on.

Thoughts will bubble up, and break,
Spilling a sea, a limpid lake,
Into the soul; and, as they go
—Lightning visitors! we know
A lattice opened, and the mind
Poised for all that is behind
The lattice, and the poising mind.

Could the memory but hold!
—All the sunsets, flushed with gold,
Are streaming in it!

All the store
Of all that ever was before
Is teeming in it!

All the wit
Of holy living, holy writ,
Waiting till we remember it,
Is dreaming in it!

JAMES STEPHENS
Theme and Variations, 1930

'...ALL GONE...'

'Age takes in pitiless hands
All one loves most away;
Peace, joy, simplicity
Where then their inward stay?'

Or so, at least they say.

'Marvel of noontide light,
Of gradual break of day;
Dreams, visions of the night
Age withers all away.'

Yes, that is what they say.

'Wonder of winter snow,
Magic of wandering moon,
The starry hosts of heaven—
Come seventy, all are gone.

'Unhappy when alone,
Nowhere at peace to be;
Drowned the old self-sown eager thoughts
Constantly stirring in thee!' . . .

Extraordinary!
That's what they *say* to me!

WALTER DE LA MARE
O Lovely England, 1953

THE PASSING DAY

A LATE lark twitters from the quiet skies;
And from the west,
Where the sun, his day's work ended,
Lingers as in content,
There falls on the old, grey city
An influence luminous and serene
A shining peace.

The smoke ascends
In a rosy-and-golden haze. The spires
Shine, and are changed. In the valley
Shadows rise. The lark sings on. The sun,
Closing his benediction,
Sinks, and the darkening air
Thrills with a sense of the triumphing night—
Night, with her train of stars
And her great gift of sleep.

So be my passing!
My task accomplished and the long day done,
My wages taken, and in my heart
Some late lark singing,
Let me be gathered to the quiet west,
The sundown splendid and serene,
Death.

W. E. HENLEY, *A Book of Verses*, 1888
(written 1876)

AFTER THE STORM

THE seas are quiet when the winds give o'er;
So calm are we when passions are no more:
For then we know how vain it was to boast
Of fleeting things, so certain to be lost:
Clouds of affection from our younger eyes
Conceal that emptiness which age descries.

The soul's dark cottage, battered and decayed,
Lets in new light through chinks that time has made
Stronger by weakness: wiser men become,
As they draw near to their eternal home:
Leaving the Old, both Worlds at once they view,
That stand upon the threshold of the New.

EDMUND WALLER, *Poems*, 1686

OLD MAN: PAINTING BY REMBRANDT VAN RIJN *c.* 1632

MOONLIGHT, CONWAY CASTLE (DETAIL): PAINTING BY J. C. IBBETSON, 1794

NIGHT-LIGHT

THE light and heat of the sun, like air and water, is a human necessity. The moon is in the nature of a luxury. She is sweetheart rather than wife. She is our night-light. The sun excites, challenges, daunts, dazzles, dazes, may even all but stun the mind with radiance. It sucks self outwards; its heat resembles a fourth skin. In its vast shimmering mantle of gold, it pours life into us.

>   With open mouth he drank the sun
>   As though it had been wine!

'Doth not the glory of the Sun pay tribute to your sight? Is not the vision of the World an amiable thing?' Not so the moon. Like a spy with a bull's-eye, she silently discloses what she shines upon. She pacifies, invites *us* in. Her light gnaws away shadow; and glides, smooth and softly as a serpent, from stone on to stone. Caught, yet unaware of being so, our instincts and our sentiments are instantly affected by her presence. 'The Sea! the Sea!' we may shout at sight of an ocean basking in splendour beneath the sun; but what barbarian would go bawling into the night to welcome the moon? We tread softly; look and think with caution; as if to be in keeping with this stealthy and motionless lustre. The preternatural is lurking near, is skulking abroad. And a beauty, or bearing, or character in things, indetectable in daylight, now lies in wait for us. Not only is every flower alone in moonlight, and many refuse to bloom until her hour draws near, not only is the air sweet and heavy with smells and odours, and every rose chilled with dew resembles a rose dreaming of itself; but even so gross and coarse a plant as the vegetable marrow, when its great thorny leaves are dusked over with the moon's silver, becomes not only singularly beautiful, but as individual an organism as a basking alligator.

WALTER DE LA MARE, *Behold, this Dreamer!* 1939

IN MY END IS MY BEGINNING

BEHOLD, I shew you a mystery: We shall not all sleep, but we shall all be changed, in a moment, in the twinkling of an eye, at the last trump: for the trumpet shall sound, and the dead shall be raised incorruptible, and we shall be changed. For this corruptible must put on incorruption, and this mortal must put on immortality. So when this corruptible shall have put on incorruption, and this mortal shall have put on immortality, then shall be brought to pass the saying that is written, Death is swallowed up in victory.

O death, where is thy sting? O grave, where is thy victory?

THE FIRST EPISTLE TO THE CORINTHIANS, XV

IF I had strength enough to hold a pen I would write how easy and pleasant a thing it is to die.

JOHN HUNTER, Surgeon,
on his deathbed, 1786

HERE lies a piece of Christ: a star in dust;
A vein of gold; a china dish that must
Be used in heaven, when God shall feast the just.

ROBERT WILD, 'An Epitaph for a Godly
Man's Tomb', *Iter Boreale*, 1668

BE STILL, MY SOUL

Be still, my soul. Consider
   The flowers and the stars.
Among these sleeping fragrances,
   Sleep now your cares.
That which the universe
   Lacks room to enclose
Lives in the folded petals
   Of this dark rose.

GERALD BULLETT, *Poems*, 1949

NOTES ON THE ILLUSTRATIONS

The names of the owners of works illustrated are printed in italics

Frontispiece FRANCIS COTES, R.A. (1725–70). Portrait of Paul Sandby, R.A., at the age of thirty-four, 1759–61. Oil on canvas. 49¼ × 39½ in. *London, Tate Gallery, by permission of the Trustees.*

17. EDGAR DEGAS (1834–1917). Woman Washing (Femme à sa toilette). *c.* 1890. Pastel drawing. 28½ × 26½ in. *Saltwood Castle, Sir Kenneth Clark, K.C.B.*

18. ROSE IN MORNING DEW. Photograph by Clarence Ponting.

25. AUGUSTUS JOHN, R.A. (b. 1879). Romilly seated. Pencil drawing. 11½ × 8½ in. Exhibited in the Augustus John Exhibition, Burlington House, 1954. *Cambridge, L. C. G. Clarke, Esq.*

26. CORNELIS DE VOS (1585–1651). Portrait of a boy. Oil on panel. 48 × 37½ in. Exhibited at the Flemish Art Exhibition, Burlington House, 1953–4. *Antwerp, Musée Mayer van den Bergh.*

35. ROELANDT SAVERY (1576–1639). Flowers and Insects. 1611. Oil on panel. 9¼ × 6¾ in. Exhibited in the Flemish Art Exhibition, Burlington House, 1953–4. *London, Mrs E. Hamilton-Brown.*

36. NEBULAE (Nebuleuse America). Telescopic photograph by George Langelaan, taken at the Haute Provence Observatory, France. *Picture Post Library.*

41. PIERRE AUGUSTE RENOIR (1841–1919). A young girl bathing. 1892. Oil on canvas. 32×25½ in. Photograph by courtesy of Dalzell Hatfield Galleries, Los Angeles. *New York, Robert Lehman, Esq.*

42. CLAUDE MONET (1840–1926). Les Peupliers. 1890. Oil on canvas. 35×28½ in. *London, Tate Gallery, by permission of the Trustees.*

47. JAN DAVIDSZ DE HEEM (1606–84). Flowers, fruit and oysters. Oil on canvas. 30×26 in. *London, Slatter Gallery.*

48. REED WARBLER. Photograph by Eric Hosking.

57. SEA SHELLS. Photograph by Edwin Smith.

58. LUTE. French, seventeenth century. *London, Victoria and Albert Museum, by permission of the Trustees.*

63. J. J. TRECK (*c.* 1606–52). Pewter, china and glass. 1649. 30× 25 in. *London, National Gallery, by permission of the Trustees.*

64. WINE GLASSES, engraved with Jacobite emblems. *c.* 1750. 6¼ in. high. Made in Newcastle. Photograph by Frederick L. Bantick. *Barham, Suffolk, Mrs John Hadfield.*

69. POMANDERS AND VINAIGRETTES, FOR CARRYING SCENT. Photograph by Edwin Smith. *London, Cameo Corner.*
    The pomanders at the top and the foot of the photograph are made of silver. The vinaigrette with chain is of gold, and the one beside it is of amethyst and gold. The oval vinaigrette is of gold and topaz.

70. TOBY JUG, known as 'The Squire'. Made by Ralph Wood, Burslem, *c.* 1770. 10¾ in. high. *London, Victoria and Albert Museum, by permission of the Trustees.*

79. ENGLISH EMBROIDERED PICTURE. Satin, embroidered with silks and seed-pearls. *c.* 1660. 11¾×9¼ in. *London, Victoria and Albert Museum, by permission of the Trustees.*

80. ARMILLARY SPHERE. A skeleton celestial globe showing the movements of the stars. Copper gilt, German, sixteenth century. 14½ in. high. *London, British Museum (Bernal Collection), by permission of the Trustees.*

85. NORBERT CASTERET AMONG STALACTITES. Photograph from *Ten Years under the Earth,* by permission of Messrs J. M. Dent & Sons.

86. KATSUSHIKA TAITŌ (*fl.* 1816–53). A carp in a pool. Coloured woodcut, Japanese. 14×6½ in. *London, Victoria and Albert Museum, by permission of the Trustees.*

91. FRANCIS TOWNE (1740–1816). Peamoor Park, near Exeter. Watercolour drawing, folded. 14½×10½ in. *Manchester, Whitworth Art Gallery, by permission of the Governors.*

92. JEAN ANTOINE WATTEAU (1684–1721). Fête in a Park. Oil on canvas. 49×74 in. *London, Wallace Collection, by permission of the Trustees.*
     The detail illustrated represents rather less than half of the painting laterally.

101. PIETER BRUEGHEL THE ELDER (?1525–69). Winter land-scape. 1565. Oil on panel. 14¾ × 22 in. Exhibited in the Flemish Art Exhibition, Burlington House, 1953–4. *Brussels, Dr F. Delporte.* The detail illustrated shows about half the picture laterally.

102. JOHN NASH, R.A. (b. 1893). The Moat, Grange Farm, Kimble. *c.* 1922. Oil on canvas. 30 × 20 in. *London, Tate Gallery, by permission of the Trustees.*

107. FRANCESCO GUARDI (1712–93). San Giorgio Maggiore. Oil on canvas. 27 × 36 in. *London, Wallace Collection, by permission of the Trustees.*
The detail illustrated represents about two-thirds of the painting.

108. LAMBETH DELFT DISH. Earthenware. *c.* 1720. 8¾ in. diameter. *London, Victoria and Albert Museum, by permission of the Trustees.*

113. QUENTIN MATSYS (1466–1530). Portrait of Aegidius, the Philosopher. Oil on panel. 29 × 20½ in. Exhibited at the Flemish Art Exhibition, Burlington House, 1953–4. *Longford Castle, The Earl of Radnor.*

114. ROBERT HAVELL (*fl.* 1810–37). The Ascent of James Sadler at Oxford, 7 July 1810. Aquatint in colours.
This ascent by Sadler, the Oxford confectioner, accompanied by his son, was to celebrate the installation of Lord Grenville as Chancellor of the University.

123. PIERRE AUGUSTE RENOIR (1841–1919). La Danse. Crayon drawing. 1883. 8 13/16 × 5 9/16 in. Exhibited at the Marlborough Gallery, London, 1953. *Bruern Abbey, The Hon. Michael Astor.*

124. JAPANESE DRAWING. Horses. Kano School. Nineteenth century. 10½ in. square. *London, Victoria and Albert Museum, by permission of the Trustees.*

129. CARLO CRIVELLI (*c.* 1430–*c.* 1495). The Annunciation. 1486. Oil on panel. 82½ × 58½ in. *London, National Gallery, by permission of the Trustees.*

The detail illustrated (actual size) is from the extreme left-hand edge of the painting. The child is looking towards the Virgin, who is kneeling in her chamber, across a courtyard beyond which are seen glimpses of varied and delightful scenes.

130. THOMAS GAINSBOROUGH, R.A. (1727–88). The Honourable Mrs Graham. 1777. Oil on canvas. 92 × 59½ inches. *Edinburgh, National Gallery of Scotland, by permission of the Trustees.*

Mrs Graham, who died in 1792 at the age of thirty-five, was perhaps the most beautiful woman to be painted by Gainsborough. This portrait sums up, in one triumphant work of art, the whole Age of Elegance.

135. SIR PETER LELY (1618–80). A Poet, in the Character of a Shepherd. *c.* 1645. Oil on canvas. 35¼ × 29¼ in. *Dulwich Art Gallery, by permission of the Trustees.*

This painting, once at Strawberry Hill, was long supposed to be an idealized portrait of Abraham Cowley, the poet.

136. CLAUDE AUGUSTIN CAYOT (1667–1722). Cupid and Psyche. 1706. Sculpture in marble. 33 in. high. *London, Wallace Collection, by permission of the Trustees.*

This charming work by a sculptor who is otherwise little known portrays Psyche as a child of the same age as the boy Cupid.

145. SIR PETER PAUL RUBENS (1577–1640). The Toilet of Venus. Oil on panel. 48×39 in. On loan exhibition at the National Gallery, London. *H.S.H. the Prince of Liechtenstein.*

146. GEORGE KNAPTON (1698–1778). Portrait of Lucy Ebberton. Oil on canvas. 29½×24½ in. *Dulwich Art Gallery, by permission of the Governors.*

151. WATCH BY EDWARD EAST. The case of gold enamelled in blue, with floral designs in white and red and landscapes in black, perhaps by Pierre Huaud, of Geneva. 2 in. diameter. *London, Victoria and Albert Museum, by permission of the Trustees.*
   Edward East, Master of the Clockmakers' Company in 1645 and 1652, was watchmaker to Charles I. It is probable that the case is rather later in date than the movement.

152. MARBLE GROUP. Probably German, eighteenth century. 16¼ in. high. *London, Victoria and Albert Museum, by permission of the Trustees.*
   This very unusual and beautifully modelled group, acquired by the Museum in 1953, presumably symbolizes Adam and Eve. The serpent's head can be seen between them. The skull is an uncommon element in such a composition.

157. EIGHTEENTH-CENTURY FANS. Photograph by Edwin Smith. *London, Mr Louis Meier.*

158. CUSHION. Embroidered in coloured silk in tent stitch (petit point). Mid-seventeenth century. 11×16 in. *London, Victoria and Albert Museum, by permission of the Trustees.*

167. GEORGE FREDERICK WATTS, R.A. (1817–1904). Choosing: a portrait of Ellen Terry. 1864. Oil on panel. 18½ × 14 in. Exhibited Royal Academy, 1864 and 1951–2. *Merstham, Kerrison Preston, Esq.*

Watts had married Ellen Terry early in 1864, when she was not quite seventeen.

168. STAFFORDSHIRE POTTERY GROUP. Salt glaze. *c.* 1740. 8 in. high. *Cambridge, Fitzwilliam Museum, by permission of the Syndics.*

173. WEDDING RING AND LOVE TOKENS. Photograph by Edwin Smith. *London, Cameo Corner.*

The gold cameo necklace and the miniature are French, of the eighteenth century. The other cameo is English, early nineteenth century.

174. LIVERPOOL DELFT DISH. *c.* 1760. 11¾ in. diameter. Photograph by courtesy of Mr. A. F. Allbrook, South Kensington. *London, Mrs J. Weston.*

179. STEFANO DA VERONA (*c.* 1375–*c.* 1440). The Virgin in the Rose Garden. Tempera on panel. *Verona, Art Gallery.*

The rose garden is the enclosed garden of the Canticle of Canticles. The Virgin is the Rose of Sharon, and is attended by Saint Catherine of Alexandria, the mystical bride of Christ. The two peacocks symbolize resurrection, and the other birds represent the souls of the faithful.

180. AMBROGIO LORENZETTI (*fl.* 1323–48). Heads of four Nuns. Fragment of fresco. *c.* 1331. 22 in. square. Formerly in the Capitolo of S. Francesco, Siena. *London, National Gallery, by permission of the Trustees.*

189. REMBRANDT VAN RIJN (1606–69). The Philosopher. *c.* 1630. Oil on panel. $21\frac{1}{2} \times 18$ in. *London, National Gallery, by permission of the Trustees.*

190. JAMES JOSEPH JACQUES TISSOT (1836–1902). Greenwich. Oil on canvas. $23\frac{1}{4} \times 31\frac{1}{2}$ in. *Bodnant, The Lord Aberconway.*
The detail illustrated shows the right-hand side of the painting.

195. RICHARD DADD (1817–87). The Fairy Feller's Masterstroke. 1858–64. Oil on canvas. 21×15 in. *Heytesbury, Siegfried Sassoon, Esq.*

This is the chief work of an extraordinary painter, who spent the greater part of his life in an asylum. It was painted during his insanity. The subject has been variously interpreted, and appears to embody the 'fire bird' theme. Mr Sacheverell Sitwell summed it up as 'an introduction to the subconscious'.

196. CHINESE POTTERY FIGURE. Man with a bird. Six dynasties period, 220–589 A.D. $8\frac{3}{4}$ in. high. *London, British Museum, by permission of the Trustees.*

201. GEARBOX OF A ROLLS-ROYCE ENGINE. Checking the main shaft on a profile machine. Photograph by Zoltan Glass.

Each gear tooth, after grinding, must be within the rigid limits of plus or minus 1/10,000 inch.

202. CASPAR NETSCHER (1639–84). The Lace-Maker. 1664. Oil on canvas. 13 × 10½ in. *London, Wallace Collection, by permission of the Trustees.*

211. PAUL GAUGUIN (1848–1903). Harvesting in Brittany. 1889. Oil on canvas. 36 × 28½ in. *London, Home House Society, by permission of the Trustees.*

212. SILVER COFFEE POT BY JOHN ELSTON. Exeter 1716. Gross weight 32 oz. Photograph by Raymond Fortt. *London, Thomas Lumley Ltd.*

217. THE WEST DOOR, CHARTRES CATHEDRAL. Photograph by Peter Pryor.

218. GRAHAM SUTHERLAND (b. 1903). Entrance to a Lane. 1939. Oil on canvas. 23½ × 19½ in. *London, Tate Gallery, by permission of the Trustees.*

223. FLEMISH ILLUMINATED MANUSCRIPT. Jean Corbechon, *Des Proprietez des Choses*, Vol. II. French translation of the *Liver de proprietatibus rerum* of Bartholomaeus Anglicus. The miniature illustrated shows the author and various birds. c. 1482. 18½ × 13½ in. *London, British Museum, by permission of the Trustees.*

224. INTERIOR OF THE CHURCH OF SAN SPIRITO, AGRIGENTO, SICILY. Photograph by Edwin Smith.

233. BED AT OCKWELLS MANOR, BERKSHIRE. Oak, with bulbous posts and arcaded back carved with strapwork. c. 1615. *Country Life* photograph, from Macquoid & Edwards' *Dictionary of English Furniture.*

234. JOSEPH MALLORD WILLIAM TURNER, R.A. (1775–1851). The Lake, from Petworth House—Sunset. *c.* 1829. Oil on canvas. 25 × 55 in. *London, Tate Gallery, by permission of the Trustees.*

The detail reproduced shows about a third of the whole painting. Until recently it has been described as a sunrise scene, but the geography of Petworth Park disproves this.

239. REMBRANDT VAN RIJN (1606–69). Portrait of an Old Man. *c.* 1632. Oil on panel. 22½ × 18½ in. Exhibited in the Loan Exhibition, Slatter Gallery, 1949. *London, George Schicht, Esq.*

240. JULIUS CAESAR IBBETSON (1759–1817). Moonlight, Conway Castle. 1794. Oil on panel. 13½ × 17½ in. *London, Victoria and Albert Museum, by permission of the Trustees.*

Endpapers: ENGHIEN TAPESTRY. Seventeenth century. In shades of green, beige, gold and brown. 16 feet 4 in. × 10 feet 4 in. *London, Vigo Art Gallery.*

INDEX OF AUTHORS AND COMPOSERS